Making Embroidered
BAGS & PURSES

Making Embroidered
BAGS & PURSES

———◆———

GISELA BANBURY AND
ANGELA DEWAR

BLANDFORD

A BLANDFORD BOOK

First published in the UK 1991
by Blandford (a Cassell imprint)
Villiers House
41/47 Strand
London WC2N 5JE

Distributed in the United States
by Sterling Publishing Co., Inc.
387 Park Avenue South, New York, NY 10016-8810

Distributed in Australia
by Capricorn Link (Australia) Pty Ltd
P.O. Box 665, Lane Cove, NSW 2066

British Library Cataloguing in Publication Data

Banbury, Gisela
    Making embroidered bags and purses.
    1. Embroidered bags & embroidered purses making
    I. Title II. Dewar, Angela
    746.9

    ISBN 0-7137-2201-0

Typeset by Litho Link Ltd., Welshpool, Powys, Wales.
Printed and bound in Spain by Graficromo.

Contents

———— ◆ ————

Acknowledgements

————◆————

The authors would like to thank the following for their generous help and encouragement: Coats Leisure Crafts Group, Evostik Adhesives and Pfaff Sewing Machines; and Clarice Blakey, Brigitt Head, Lucy Koppelmann, Sheenadh Martin, Margaret Rivers and Margaret Swain.

We would also like to thank the following embroiderers for lending us their work, which is illustrated in the colour photographs: Mary Anderson (shell purse, page 25); Clarice Blakey (*or nué* evening bag, page 122); Diana Byers (tennis ball evening bag, page 81); Mary Carroll (canvaswork shoulder bag with leather trimmings, page 51); Hazel Credland (clutch-style evening bag, page 81); Janet Edmonds (silk drawstring bag, page 69); Janet Edwards (triangular neck purse, page 21); Kate Farrow (thatched cottage purse, page 25); Simone Fruin (box-shaped evening bag, page 81); Frances Gibb (bridesmaid's drawstring bag and silk evening bag, pages 76 and 81); Claire Johnson (dragon evening bag, page 80); Rosemary Lemon (smocked silk evening bag, page 88); Frances Minter (silk neck purse and drawstring bag in trapunto quilting, pages 21 and 76); Beryl Morgan (goldwork evening bag, page 85); Delia Pusey (evening bag in roller-printed fabric, page 85); Valerie Riley (canvaswork bag with leather trimming and lurex and black poplin evening bags, pages 51 and 69, above and below); Margaret Rivers (silk and canvaswork bag, page 89); Sheila Shaw (fish scale bag, page 88); Jane Smith (smocked drawstring bag and smocked pouch, pages 76 and 122); Jane Walter (sports bag, page 92); Jean Wilson (umbrella beach bag, page 92).

And finally we would like to thank Frances Gibb for her drawings (diagrams 102, 103 and 105).

Introduction

◆

ARE you an embroiderer who enjoys making beautiful and useful objects? Then this book is for you.

In the following pages you will find instructions for making a variety of embroidered containers – for want of a better all-purpose word. The projects have been designed to help you to achieve a smart and crisp finish. Many different embroidery techniques have been employed, and the construction methods range from the very simple to the intricate, which will suit all abilities. Advice is given on the use of easily obtainable, strong clasps and frames, which will give your work a professional look. It is well worth spending time and only a little money to order these from the suppliers listed at the back of the book. It would be a pity to spoil a beautifully embroidered bag by giving scant attention to planning and basic necessities such as a reliable strap or closure.

To avoid repeating common techniques such as stretching an embroidered canvas or making tassels, they have been put into a chapter by themselves (Chapter 8). Some of the materials are referred to by their trade name but, if your local supplier doesn't stock these particular makes, there is a description of the materials on page 116.

Projects

All the projects in the book have been designed to be made in the simplest way possible.

It is important to read through a project before beginning work. A list of requirements is given at the start, so do try to have everything to hand before you begin. This saves time and frustration. We strongly recommend that every project should first be made as a mock up in any spare cotton fabric. Make sure that the instructions are fully understood. It is not necessary to put in all the finishing touches at this stage, such as stiffening, clasps, closures and handles or straps. The idea is to make yourself familiar with the pattern and to understand the construction; in other words, make a practice piece. All measurements are given in both inches and centimetres, but the two are not interchangeable.

In addition to the projects, you will find in the book photographs of colourful designs that should stimulate your imagination and encourage you to enrich your talent and find your own style. We hope that after successfully completing some of the projects you will feel confident enough to tackle your own design ideas.

Glasses Cases

GLASSES should be kept in one of two places: either at the end of your nose, or, if not in use, in a glasses or spectacle case. When you bring out your spectacles at a candle-lit restaurant table, to be able to read the menu, do you lay your glasses case on the table? Does it match your dress or handbag? Does it bring out the colour of your eyes? Or is it one of those greyish containers that usually live in the kitchen drawer, near your recipe books, with floury fingerprints all over it?

If the latter is the situation, it is time you spent a few evenings making yourself an attractive case for your spectacles. A glasses case is not only meant to look pretty. There is a practical side to it as well: it should protect your glasses from getting dirty and prevent the lenses from becoming scratched and the frame from bending or breaking. To do this, your glasses case should be of the correct size for your glasses, should be soft and smooth on the inside, and the outside should hold its shape and stand up to frequent handling.

OPPOSITE
Glasses cases worked in a variety of embroidery techniques. Top row, left to right: *automatic machine embroidery worked on corduroy with the Pfaff CD Creative sewing machine; machined patchwork and quilting, using Liberty lawns and silks; and triple leviathan stitch on canvas sewn into a metal frame.* Bottom row, left to right: *project 1 – a glasses case worked in bargello; a cross stitch pattern worked on even-weave cotton with contrasting binding; and project 2 – an embroidered glasses case with a spring frame.*

A Glasses Case Worked in Bargello

Bargello is a variety of canvaswork, sometimes also known as flame stitch, Florentine stitch, Irish stitch or Hungarian point. It is worked in an upright stitch over a stiff single canvas. The canvas will give strength and shape to the glasses case, while the soft yarns and smooth stitches will add all the padding necessary to protect the glasses within.

To make sure that your glasses case is the right size for your glasses, you have to make a paper mock up first.

Making a Paper Mock up

You will need the following.

MATERIALS

- 1 piece of A4 paper
- Paper scissors
- A few pins
- Your glasses

The paper should be 1in (2.5cm) wider than your glasses; cut it to size if necessary. Wrap the paper loosely once around your folded glasses, and pin it together on the long side (see diagram 1).

Your glasses should be completely covered by this paper tube, but they should slide in and out very easily. Cut off the surplus paper. Take your glasses out and close one of the short sides of the paper tube with a pin (see diagram 2).

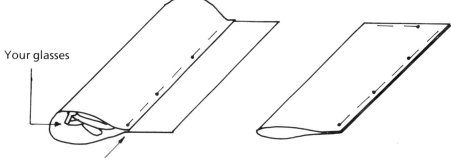

Your glasses

Cut here, close to pins

1 *Making a paper pattern for a glasses case; step 1*

2 *Making a paper pattern for a glasses case; step 2*

Check (a) that your glasses really slide easily in and out of the paper mock up, and (b) that they are covered completely when they are in the paper mock up. Take all the pins out. Unfold your paper and check that the four corners of the paper are at right angles. If you started with an oblong and you folded your paper carefully around your glasses with sides matching, the corners should still be at right angles.

You now have in front of you a paper pattern without seam allowance for a case for your own glasses. The piece of paper represents the shape and size of the area you are to embroider. The paper pattern for our case turned out to be 6 × 6in (15 × 15cm) square.

Working the Glasses Case

To work the glasses case shown in the photograph on page 8, which measures 6 × 3in (15 × 7.5cm), you will need the following.

MATERIALS

- 1 piece of single canvas with 16 threads to the inch (2.5cm), 8 × 8in (20 × 20cm)
- 1 piece of heavy, smooth, silky lining material, 6¾ × 6¾in (17 × 17cm)
- 2 skeins each of DMC tapisserie wool Nos. 7191, 7192 and 7951
- 2 skeins each of DMC stranded cotton Nos. 501 and 503

NEEDLEWORK SKILLS INVOLVED

- Bargello stitch
- Oversewing
- Slip stitch

Preparing the Canvas

Adding a seam allowance of 1in (2.5cm) on all four sides of our paper pattern, we enlarged the size of our piece of canvas to 8 × 8in (20 × 20cm). For your own glasses case choose a good quality single canvas with 16 threads to the inch (2.5cm). Bind the edges with masking tape to prevent your yarn getting caught on the rough canvas while you work.

Working the Embroidery

The mixture of wool and cotton threads chosen, dull and shiny, gives a lively effect.

Thread your needle with DMC tapisserie wool No. 7951. Find the centre line of your canvas by folding it in half. Start the bargello pattern as shown in diagram 3, working over four threads, with the first stitch worked 1in (2.5cm) from the left-hand edge of the canvas and sitting on the centre line. Work the pattern over the back of the glasses case as shown, until you reach

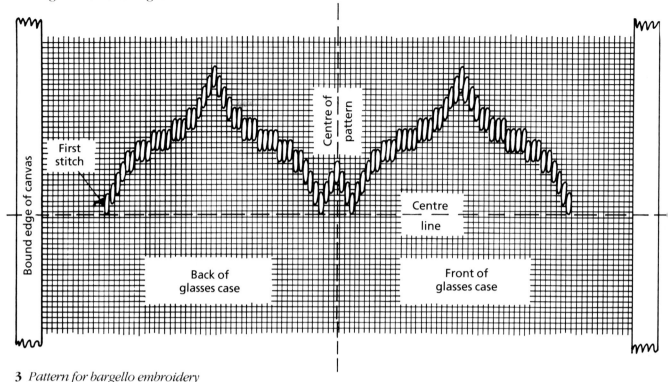

3 *Pattern for bargello embroidery*

the centre of the pattern. Then continue over the front of the case, working the pattern in mirror image as shown. The pattern line should come to an end about 1in (2.5cm) from the right-hand edge of the canvas.

Now thread your needle with two lengths of DMC stranded cotton No. 501. Each length of stranded cotton is made up of six fine, individual strands, so you now have twelve strands of stranded cotton in your needle. Work your next row of bargello stitches below the first one, following the ups and downs of the pattern correctly, but working over only two threads of the canvas, creating a narrower line of stitching.

Using DMC tapisserie wool, first No. 7191, then No. 7192, work two more rows of stitches below the others, both over four threads of the canvas. With two lengths of DMC stranded cotton No. 503 in your needle, work one row of stitches below the others, but over two threads of canvas only.

Repeat from the first row, working down towards the bottom edge of the canvas. When you are 1in (2.5cm) from the bottom edge of the canvas, even out the pattern into a straight line.

Now work from your first line of stitches towards the top edge of the canvas, alternating colours and size of stitches as required. When the points of the bargello design are 6in (15cm) from the bottom edge of the embroidery, start evening out the pattern to a straight line. You may work the colour changes to the very last line of the embroidery, or you may fill in the corners of the bargello pattern with one colour only, as shown on page 8.

Your embroidery should now cover a square measuring 6 × 6in (15 × 15cm).

Stretching the Canvas

Cover a clean board with a damp, soft towel. Lay your embroidery face down on the damp cloth and pin it into place with stainless steel drawing pins as described in Chapter 8. Make sure your canvas remains square and does not get distorted. Leave this until the towel is completely dry and the canvas is stiff again. Do not hurry this process, which may take up to a week or longer.

Making Up the Glasses Case

Trim your canvas seam allowance to ten threads all around, turning eight threads to the reverse side, and leaving two threads showing on the right side. Fold your embroidery in half along the spine of the glasses case. Close the seam as shown in diagram 4, starting at point A and working towards point B with oversewing stitches, using two colours of DMC tapisserie wool alternately. Open the case at point B and finish the remaining single edge in the same way, until you reach point B again. Finish off.

Lining

Use a smooth, silky fabric in a toning colour, and cut a square, measuring 6¾ × 6¾in (17 × 17cm). Taking ½in (1cm) seam allowance, make up a bag in exactly the same shape as the embroidered glasses case. Push the lining inside the case, wrong sides together. Fold in the lining seam allowance around the top edge and slip stitch neatly to the oversewn edge (see Chapter 8, diagram 95).

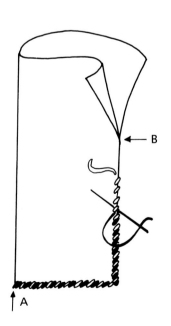

4 *Stitching up the glasses case*

An Embroidered Glasses Case on a Spring Frame

To make the glasses case shown on page 8, which measures 6¾ × 3¼in (17.5 × 8.5cm), you will need the following.

MATERIALS

- 1 piece of evenweave cotton with 18 threads to the inch (2.5cm), 4 × 16in (10 × 40cm)
- 1 ball Anchor pearl cotton (coton perlé) No. 5 in the colour of your choice (you will only use part of this)
- 2yd (2m) of Anchor pearl cotton (coton perlé) No. 5 in a contrasting colour or of a metallic thread
- 1 piece of silk lining material, 4 × 14in (10 × 35cm)
- 1 piece of padding (Domette, thin wadding, towelling or thin foam), 4 × 11½in (10 × 28cm)
- 1 spring frame
- 1 tapestry needle No. 18 or 20
- Some sewing cotton

NEEDLEWORK SKILLS INVOLVED

- Cross stitch
- Backstitch
- Herringbone stitch (optional)
- Straight machine stitching or hand sewing
- Oversewing
- Hemming by hand

Preparing the Fabric

Oversew all raw edges, to prevent them from fraying. Mark the centre line of all pieces of material as shown in diagram 5.

Working the Embroidery

Follow the chart in diagram 6, starting the embroidery eight threads to the right or left of the centre line marked. The larger cross stitches and the backstitches are worked over three threads; the smaller cross stitches are worked over two threads. When the embroidery is finished, press the fabric on the wrong side, under a damp cloth and with a medium hot iron.

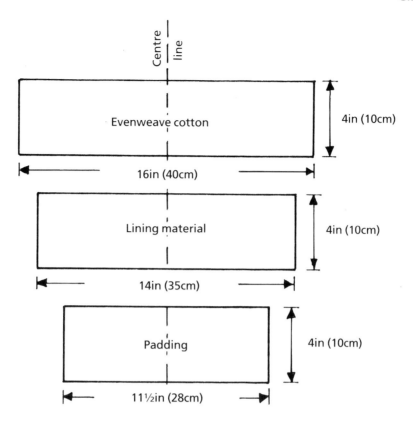

5 *Pattern for cross stitch glasses case*

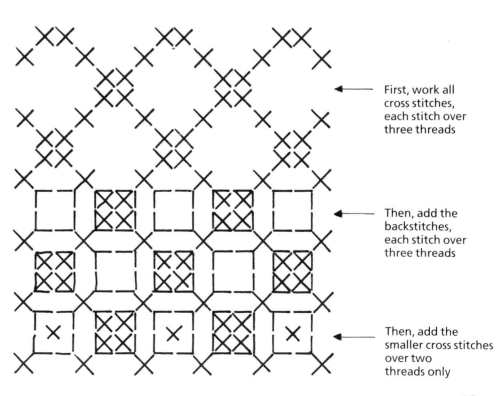

First, work all cross stitches, each stitch over three threads

Then, add the backstitches, each stitch over three threads

Then, add the smaller cross stitches over two threads only

6 *Cross stitch pattern for glasses case*

15

Making the Outer Pouch

Fold the embroidered fabric along the centre line, right sides together. Close 6in (15cm) of the two long side seams. You may use the machine or sew by hand. The seam should run eight threads away from the edge of the embroidery. Turn the pouch right side out.

Sewing in the Spring Frame

Wrap one of the loose ends of the pouch around one shank of the spring frame, so that the overall length of the case is about 6½in (17cm). Sew this hem invisibly (see Chapter 8 for slip stitching). Repeat with the second shank of the spring frame. Make sure you use the shanks the right way round, so that they slot into each other when you come to insert the pins.

Making up the Lining

Match the centre line of the padding with that of the lining and machine or hand sew them together along that line. Fold the two fabrics in half along this seam, with the lining on the inside. Close the two long sides as far as the padding, taking ½in (1cm) seam allowance. Trim the seam allowance of the padding back to the stitch line.

Finishing the Glasses Case

Fit the lining pouch into the embroidered pouch; a ruler may be helpful. At the top edge, fold the lining to the wrong side, so that the fold line comes to lie at your row of hem stitching at the bottom edge of the spring frame. Attach the lining to the outer fabric, either invisibly or with a decorative stitch such as herringbone stitch (see Chapter 8 for herringbone stitch).

Slot the two shanks of the spring frame together and insert the two pins, one in each side. With a pair of pliers or a small hammer squash the centre part of the joins a little to stop the pins from falling out.

Purses

WHERE do you keep small amounts of change? Perhaps in a little pile on the window-sill. It would be safer in a purse. Your children's pocket money would be less likely to get lost or mislaid if it were kept in something like a neck purse, for instance. Since purses are as much fun to make as they are to give or to receive as a present, nobody in your family should be able to say: 'I haven't got a purse.'

There is no limit to the possible designs for purses. As long as they are coin proof and big or small enough to hold your change, you can make them any shape you like, from a house to a hot air balloon.

The fastener on a purse has to be secure and reliable. For the purses shown in the following pages we have used three varieties of fasteners, all easily available – zips, spring frames and twist knob frames (see suppliers list).

To decorate a purse, any embroidery technique is suitable. Fine, delicate work like *or nué*, gold work, bead work, lace, drawn thread work and cut work make beautiful evening purses, and the open work techniques will be enhanced by contrasting linings.

Purses for children and for everyday use have to withstand more vigorous handling and are therefore better worked on tougher fabrics. Canvaswork, appliqué, patchwork and quilting are quite suitable as decoration.

Purses with long cords can be hung around the neck as fashion accessories or tucked away for security.

Often purses are made to match a larger bag. Since they are small items, they do not take too long to finish, but offer plenty of scope to the adventurous embroiderer as well as to the beginner.

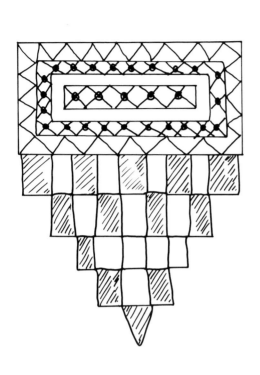

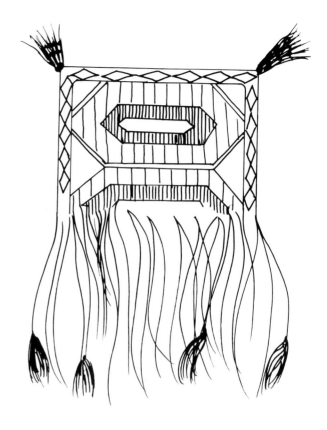

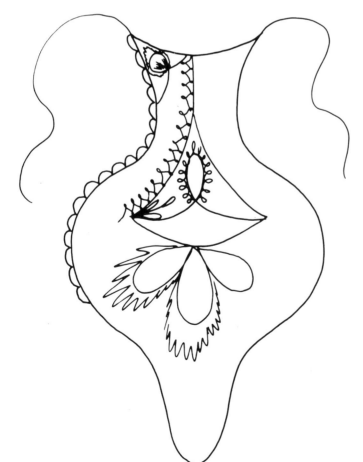

TOP LEFT

7 *Studying work from all parts of the world can be an inspiration for all kinds of embroidery. This purse is from Cuba. Detached patches, joined only at their corners, form a deep, pointed fringe, and the top is embroidered with herringbone stitch and needleweaving.*

TOP RIGHT

8 *This Peruvian bag could be interpreted in several ways – with wrapped cords, or in appliqué or patchwork, for example.*

LEFT

9 *An unusually shaped bag from Portugal is embroidered with Cretan stitch and with long and short stitch, and it has a braided edge.*

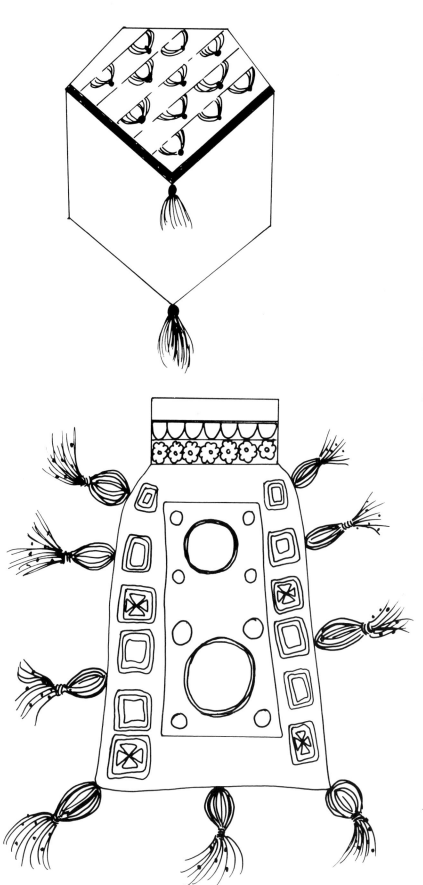

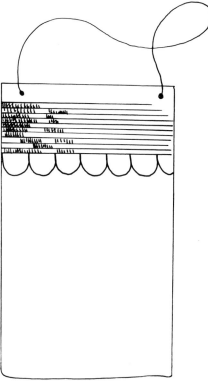

TOP LEFT

10 *The eye-catching flap of this seven-sided bag from Turkey is made from strips of fabric with tassels inserted into the seams. The beaded heads of the tassels are allowed to hang loosely, while the fringed ends are trapped in the seams.*

TOP RIGHT

11 *This Russian bag has a deep border made from red and navy blue wrapped cords.*

LEFT

12 *This little bag from Pakistan is decorated with Shi-sha glass, which is typical of the area, and with rows of chain stitch worked in brightly coloured yarns. The tassels around the edge are further embellished with small, shiny beads.*

A Cross Stitch Purse on a Metal Frame

To make the purse shown in the photograph on page 21 you will need the following.

MATERIALS

- 1 piece of fabric, approx. 6 × 8in (15 × 20cm) of either evenweave cotton, with 22 threads to the inch (2.5cm), or Aida cloth, with 11 or 14 threads to the inch (2.5cm)
- 1 piece of lining material, 6 × 8in (15 × 20cm)
- 1 metal frame with a bar length of 2½in (6.5cm)
- 1 ball Anchor pearl cotton (cotton perlé) No. 8 in a contrasting colour to your fabric
- 1 tapestry needle No. 18

NEEDLEWORK SKILLS INVOLVED

- **Cross stitch worked following a chart**
- **Straight machine stitching**
- **Zigzag machine stitching or oversewing by hand**

Preparing the Fabric for Embroidery

To stop the fabric fraying, secure the raw edges with oversewing or zigzag machining.

Copy the paper pattern given in diagram 13 on to a piece of firm paper and cut it out. Pin this pattern to one half of your fabric, and mark the outline of the pattern on the fabric by running a line of tacking stitches around it.

Working the Embroidery

If you are using evenweave fabric with 22 threads to the inch (2.5cm), the cross stitches are worked over two threads; if you are using Aida cloth, each stitch is worked over one group of threads. Work the design, following the chart in diagram 14 accurately. Make sure that the centre line of the design matches the centre line of your marked semicircle. Secure all thread ends by darning them into the back of the embroidery.

OPPOSITE

Top: *project 3 – a purse worked in cross stitch on a metal frame;* centre right: *a silk neck purse in San Blas patchwork with decorative beaded tassels;* below right: *a canvaswork neck purse with an embroidered butterfly and hand-twisted cord;* and left: *a triangular neck purse in free machine embroidery.*

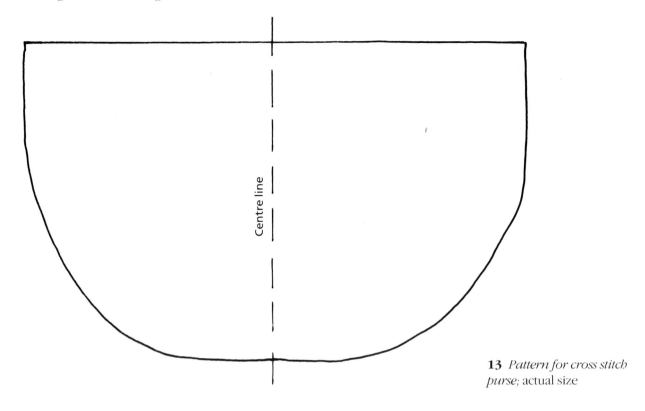

13 *Pattern for cross stitch purse;* actual size

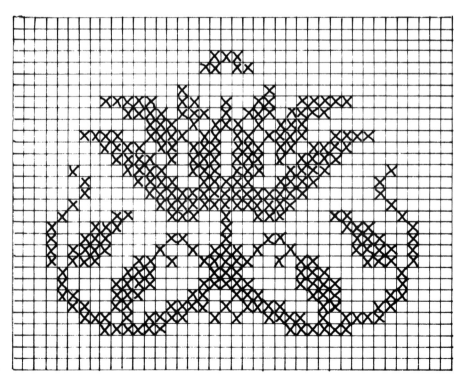

14 *Cross stitch pattern for purse*

Making the Purse

Add ½in (1cm) seam allowance to the curved outline and cut out the semicircle. Place this, with the embroidery face down, on the second half of your fabric and, using it as a guide, cut out a second semicircle. Fold your lining material in half, right sides together, and cut two semicircles for the lining of the purse. Place these on the wrong side of the embroidery, with the plain piece of fabric at the bottom of this sandwich. Taking ½in (1cm) seam allowance, machine around the curved edge with straight stitches. Trim and clip the seam allowance as shown in diagram 15. Slip the fabric at the bottom of the swatch over the other three, thus turning the purse right side out and exposing the embroidery. Pull the purse into shape and open the pouch.

Neaten the top edge of the pouch either by oversewing by hand or by machining with a close zigzag stitch, working through both lining and outer fabric.

Fitting the Purse to the Frame

Mark the centre of the straight edge of the semicircular pouch on the front and back. Open out the frame fully and push the zigzagged edge of the

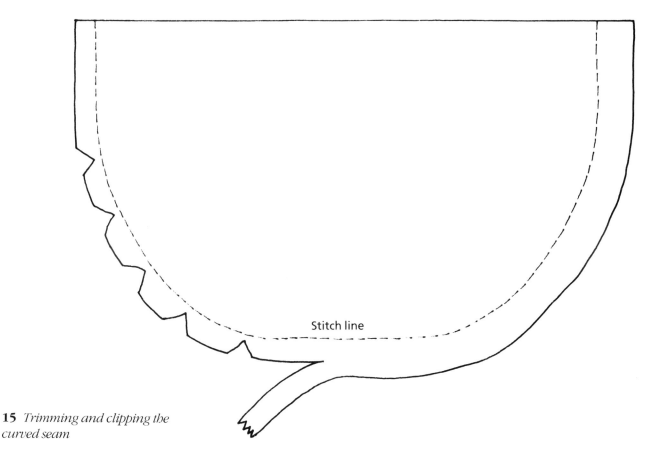

Stitch line

15 *Trimming and clipping the curved seam*

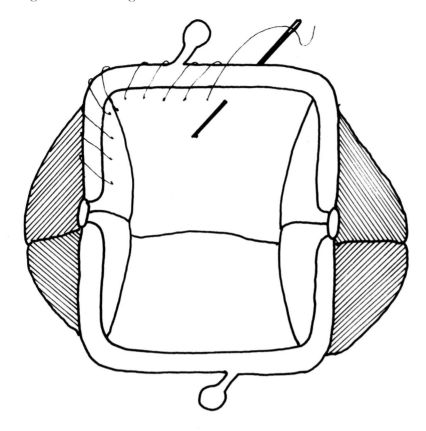

16 *Tacking the purse into the frame, ready for pinching*

pouch into the groove of the frame, matching the centres of the fabric with the centres of the frame. The side seam should meet the hinges, and any slack fabric should be worked into pleats in the four corners of the frame.

With only two hands it is almost impossible to keep everything in place! Help yourself by tacking through the fabric and over the frame, as shown in diagram 16, to keep the pouch in the groove of the frame. The tacking will enable you to manoeuvre the fabric to some extent, allowing you to arrange the folds and pleats evenly and to check that your purse closes easily.

You now have to press the shanks of the frame together, trapping the fabric in between. You can do this either in a vice or with a small hammer. Whichever way you choose, you will have to protect the polished surface of the frame from damage by placing it between some pieces of card. If you use a vice, take care not to damage the hinges or fasteners. If you use a hammer, open the purse fully and place the corner of the frame on a piece of card on the corner of a table. Now, placing a piece of wood about the size of a domino on to the shanks of the frame, start hammering them together. Do this little by little, going round and round again, to press the frame evenly, without distorting it. Check that the pouch of the purse is secure in the frame before taking the tacking stitches out.

OPPOSITE
Purses worked in a variety of embroidery techniques. Top left: *a shell purse worked with rich stitchery in delicate colours on fine canvas;* top right: *a thatched cottage purse in free hand embroidery on linen, closed with a spring frame;* below left: *tent, cross and tufted stitch on canvas on a spring frame; and* below right: *project 4 – a machine-embroidered silk shell purse on a spring frame.*

A Machine-embroidered Silk Shell Purse on a Spring Frame

Read through all the instructions before you begin the purse. To work the purse shown in the photograph on page 25, which measures 5 × 5in (13 × 13cm), you will need the following.

MATERIALS

- 1 purse spring frame (see suppliers list)
- 1 piece of shell pink silk, approx. 9in (25cm) of 36in (90cm) width fabric
- 1 piece of lining fabric, approx. 9in (25cm) of 36in (90cm) width fabric
- 1 piece of heavy sew-in Vilene, approx. 8 × 12in (20 × 30cm)
- 1 piece Domette, at least 10 × 10in (25 × 25cm)
- 20in (50cm) of thin string
- 1 skein of pale pink Coats Anchor stranded embroidery cotton
- Approx. 24 seed pearl beads
- Sewing thread for the machining to match your silk fabric
- Coats machine embroidery thread, a deeper colour than your silk fabric
- 1 small tambour frame, 6–8in (15–20cm) in diameter
- Marker pen or HB pencil
- Fine paint brush
- Adhesive (PVA or Evostik Impact 2)

NEEDLEWORK SKILLS INVOLVED

- Straight machine stitching
- Machine whip stitch
- Piping
- Stab stitch

Preparing the Fabric for Machine Embroidery

First, make a paper pattern, using diagram 17 as your guide. Note: the pattern is not drawn with a seam allowance. Lay the pattern on the Vilene twice and draw around it carefully. Cut around the two shapes, just inside the lines, so that the Vilene shapes are a little smaller than the pattern.

Lay your pattern on the right side of the silk, again twice, but leaving at

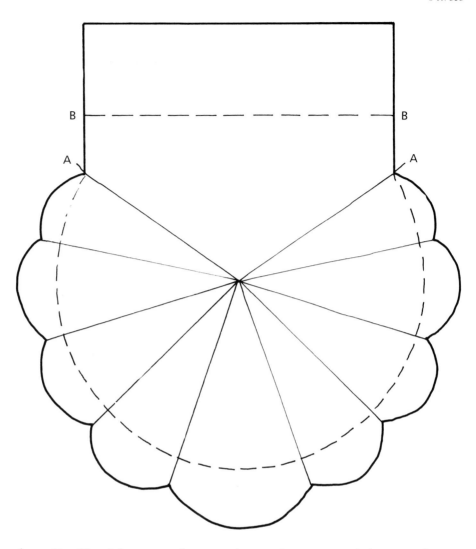

17 *Pattern for shell purse;*
actual size

least 2in (5cm) between the two shapes. Draw around them. With your sewing machine, stay stitch very carefully round the shell shapes on the drawn line. Use a marker pen to draw in the lines of the design.

Place one of the silk outlines over the Domette and tack the two fabrics together (see diagram 18).

Framing the Fabric for Machining

Stretch the silk/Domette into a small tambour frame; it must be really tight. The Domette side must lie flat on the table, with the silk on top (see diagram 19).

Machining

First, stitch the lines of the design, carrying your stitching beyond the edges.

Work an area of whip stitch in a free vermicelli pattern into the upper section of the shell, using machine embroidery thread. To work whip stitch,

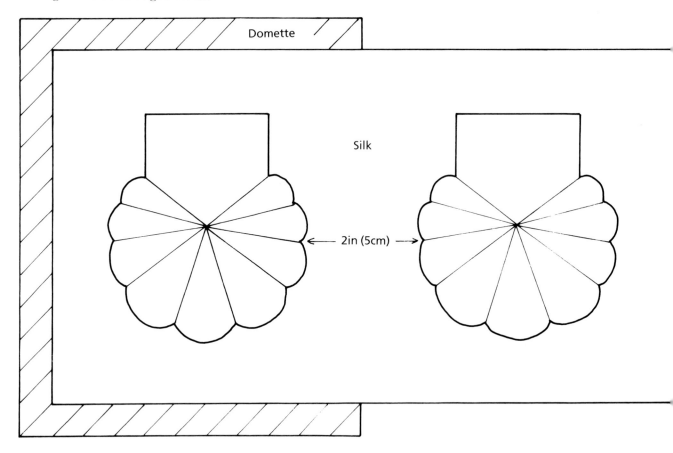

18 *Backing the silk shape with Domette*

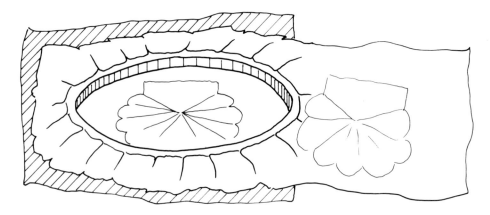

19 *Fixing the fabric into a tambour frame*
(see also page 126)

lower the feed on the machine and remove the presser foot. Loosen the tension of the spool case by turning the small screw on the spring a few times. Tighten the upper tension. Adjusting the tensions in this way will bring up the bottom thread and result in a raised, textured line of stitching. Practise on some spare bits of your fabric before working on your purse. Machine techniques are always a matter of trial and error, as all machines vary in their response to tension changes. It is a good idea to keep a separate spool case for machine embroidery. Identify it with a dab of red nail polish.

Put the frame under the needle and lower the needle into the fabric. Don't forget to put down the tension lever, even though the foot is not in use. Draw up the bottom thread and work a couple of stitches on the spot to anchor the threads. Now begin to sew, moving the frame as you go. By running the machine quite fast and moving the frame in a circular motion you can make attractive spirals while you take your line of thread for a walk!

Sewing on the Seed Pearls

When the machine embroidery is completed, trim away the Domette to the stay stitching. Sew some pearls over the whip stitching in a random fashion and then work some small French knots in the same way (see Chapter 8, diagram 88).

Cutting Out the Purse

Allowing a seam turning of about ½in (1cm), cut out both the silk shell shapes. Using the tip of the paint brush, touch the entire edge of the shapes with some adhesive, which can be diluted with a little water to make it flow more easily. Do this also on the seam allowance of the V-shaped indentations of the scallops. Allow to dry. The adhesive will prevent the silk from fraying while you work on it.

Covering the Vilene Shells

Spread a small amount of adhesive in a band about ¼in (5mm) wide around the edge of the Vilene shapes. Lay the Vilene shapes, glue side uppermost, on the wrong side of the silk shape. Now, working on one scallop at a time and snipping into each V as you reach it, fold over the silk seam allowance and press it firmly to the glued Vilene. Use your clean fingers to press and ease it into a good, smooth shape. Repeat the whole process with the second shell shape. Turn under the seam allowances at the sides of the top flaps and press.

Piping

Make a length of very fine silk piping with a seam allowance of ¼in (5mm), (see Chapter 8 for piping).

Because it would be difficult to pipe such an intricate shape with stitching, it is easier to glue the piping in place. The scallop shapes are emphasized afterwards with a few tight little stitches over each V. Proceed as follows. Spread a small amount of adhesive on to the seam allowance of the piping. Take the embroidered shell and, beginning at point B (see diagram 17), press the piping to the wrong side, with the piping edge protruding just beyond the shell edge. Continue around all the scallops, clipping the seam allowance of the piping to the stitch line as you reach each V. This will enable you to bend the piping around the sharp corners. Finish at B and taper the piping away, under the shape. You can remove a little of the piping cord at these points to keep the purse as flat and neat as possible. Push back the covering fabric by about ¼in (5mm) and snip off a little of the string. Pull the fabric up again and push it away, as described. When all the scallops are piped, leave the glue to dry. Sharpen up the shell shape by hand stitching over the piping at each V several times.

Sewing in the Spring Frame

Take one half of your spring frame and fold over it the top flap of the embroidered shell at B (see diagram 17). Hand stitch the raw edge to the Vilene. Take the plain shell and fold and stitch it over the other half of the spring frame, making sure you have the spring the right way round, so that a hinge is formed when both halves slot together.

Joining the Shell Halves Together

The two shells can now be stitched together invisibly by stab stitching through the folded edges of the front and back. Working from the front, push your needle into the ditch, where the piping and shell are joined, and slip it into the folded edge of the back before bringing it through to the front again.

Lining

The broken line in diagram 17 indicates the stitch line for the lining of the purse. Add ¼in (5mm) turning to this and cut out two lining shapes. With right sides together, stitch around the edge, up to A. Fold under the top flaps. Push the lining into the purse and hem the folded top edges to the purse flaps inside the frame.

Finishing Off

Sew a pearl on each V, passing your thread inside the piping after each bead, to avoid too much fastening off. Insert the pins provided through the hinge at each side of the frame and hammer them into place with a light knock.

Bags for
Special Occasions

THERE will come a day to all of us when, instead of going to work in the usual humdrum way, we will dress up in our finery, perhaps in a new outfit for the occasion, and go out for the day. Our everyday handbag will not be good enough. It may not go with the dress, and it most likely will be too big. A special bag is needed for a special occasion. Often a clutch bag will answer this need. Choose a simple construction and an unfussy shape, which lend themselves very well to embroidered decoration. The bag can be made to match a particular outfit by using the same fabrics, or by matching or toning the colours. To get away from traditional looks, try unusual combinations, such as silk with calico, and do not be afraid to use leather.

It is unwise to spend hours on a piece of embroidery and then to try to design a bag to accommodate it. You may end up with a bag you don't really like. Plan the bag first, establish the construction and sequence of work, and then choose a suitable embroidery technique. This will save a lot of time and headache.

When it comes to the mechanics of the bag, the fastening, do not take the lazy way out. That button that you have had lying around for some time or that bit of velcro you can buy in the high street can be improved upon. It is very difficult to open velcro unobtrusively – everybody will be able to hear you rip your bag open. Look for a proper handbag fastener. Make a matching button or tassel specially, or buy a zip, a magnetic press-stud or a twistknob lock (see suppliers list). You will know what you will need at the planning stage, so order it then, and it will have arrived long before you have finished the embroidery.

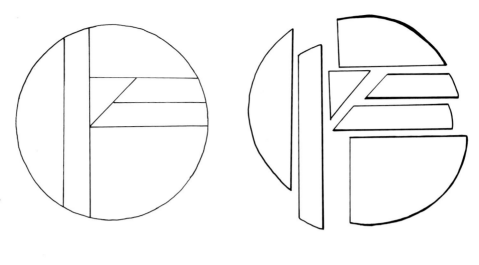

20 *Dividing and re-arranging a circle*

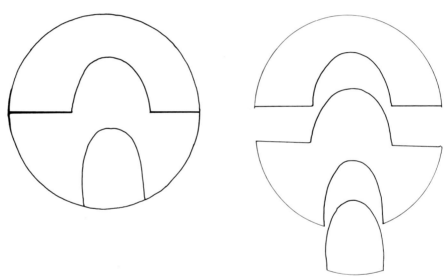

21 *This method of design, using cut paper and collage technique, gave the idea for the decorated flap of the bag on page 37*

22 *The shape of the bag flap cut out and re-arranged to obtain a pleasing design*

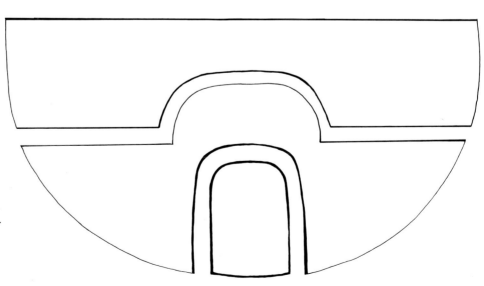

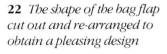

OPPOSITE
A waistcoat and matching shoulder bag. A rich brocade was used for both the waistcoat and the bag, and the pattern of the material was emphasized on the bag with quilting and French knots.

A Simple Clutch Bag with Double Gusset

To make the clutch bag shown on page 37, which measures approximately 12 × 6in (30 × 15cm), you will need the following.

MATERIALS

- 27in (75cm) of a firm cotton, such as twill, 36 or 45in (90 or 115cm) wide (if you decide on a different decoration which does not include tucks, 18in (50cm) will be sufficient)
- Cotton lining fabric, approx. 18 × 18in (46 × 46cm)
- 1 piece of heavy sew-in Vilene, approx. 18 × 13in (46 × 33cm)
- 1 piece of foam, ¼in (5mm) thick, 18 × 13in (46 × 33cm)
- 2 pieces of card, 1 × 1in (2.5 × 2.5cm)
- 1 magnetic press-stud
- Thread to match your cotton fabric
- Adhesive (Evostik Impact 2)
- Approx. 40in (1m) piping

NEEDLEWORK SKILLS INVOLVED

- Tailor's tacks
- Piping
- Machined tucks
- One machine embroidery stitch (automatic)
- Slip stitch

Working the Embroidery

Cut a piece of cotton twill, measuring 13 × 18in (33 × 46cm). Beginning at one of the narrow ends of the strip, create an alternating pattern with rows of machine tucks and automatic embroidery stitches as shown on page 37. When you have completed an area of about 6in (15cm), press your work and lay it on a flat surface to cut out the bag.

Cutting Out the Bag

Make paper patterns following diagrams 23 and 24. Pin the paper pattern for the bag to the cotton twill, the wider end on the embroidery. Allow for a seam of ½in (1cm) and cut out the bag. Transfer the fold lines and points B1 to the fabric with tailor's tacks. Adding the same seam allowance as before, cut two gussets against the fold from the remaining fabric (see diagram 25).

Cut out the Vilene to the same size as the bag and tack it to the wrong side of the bag.

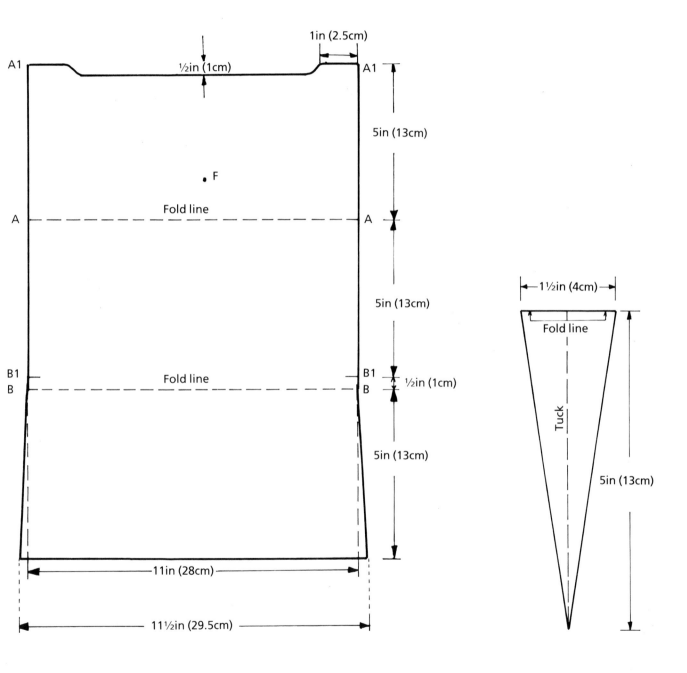

23 *Pattern for clutch bag*

24 *Pattern for gusset*

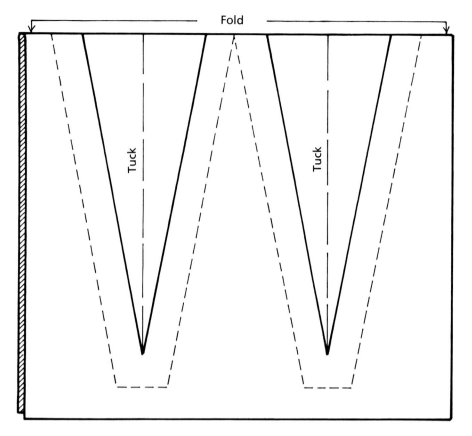

25 *Lay out for the gusset*

26 *Edge stitching the gusset*

Piping

Apply a length of narrow piping to the edge A1–A1 and to the flap section B–B (see Chapter 8 for piping).

Gussets

Crease the folded gussets along the centre line and machine stitch close to the fold through all four layers of fabric as shown in diagram 26. This pin tuck will prevent the gusset from poking out at the sides of the bag. Treat the tuck side as the wrong side of the gussets.

Sewing in the Gussets

Make a ½in (1cm) line of stay stitching through points A (see diagram 23). Clip to the stay stitching at these points. Insert the gussets by machine, right sides together, beginning at A1, pivoting the seam at point A and finishing at point B1.

Trim away the Vilene on the seam allowance, close to the stitching.

OPPOSITE

Bags for special occasions. From the top: a silk and leather patchwork bag with press-stud closure; project 5 – a simple clutch bag with a double gusset; a semicircular bag with silk and leather appliqué on the flap; and a bag worked using the Pfaff CD Creative sewing machine in automatic machine stitching on black and white cotton ticking.

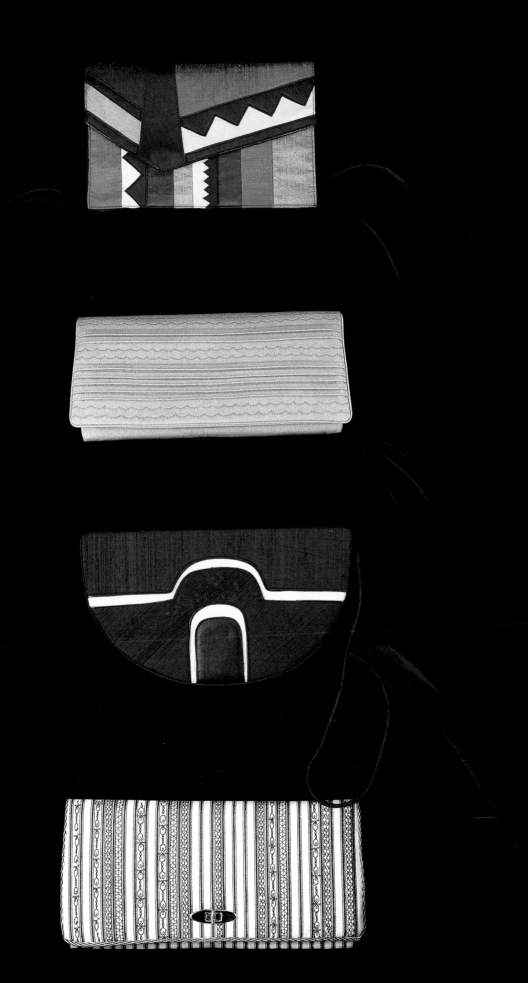

Foam Interlining

Cut a piece of foam, very slightly smaller than the front rectangle A1–A1, A–A. Angle the scissors to bevel the edges of the foam. Stick the foam, bevelled side down, to the wrong side of the front of the bag.

Cut another rectangle of foam for the back, A–A, B1–B1. Trim and fix this rectangle as before. Repeat with the flap section, noting that this is not a rectangle, but a trapezium.

Press-stud, Receiving End

Make two small cuts in one of the pieces of card, spaced to fit the prongs of the fastener. Locate point F on the front of the bag (see diagram 23). Make two small holes either side of F, spacing them to take the fastener. Push the prongs, from the front to the back, through all thicknesses of materials and through the card. Fold the prongs outwards and back against the card. Lightly knock them flat with a small hammer.

Lining

Cut out the lining, using the original paper pattern. Stay stitch the curved front edge, A1–A1. Clip the curves to the stay stitching. Place the flaps of the bag and the lining right sides together and pin. Machine stitch around the flap from point B on one side to point B on the other. Trim away the Vilene seam allowance close to the stitching and trim the corners.

Turn the flap section right side out.

Press all the remaining seam allowances on the lining to the wrong side.

Press-stud, Stud Half

Fold the flap down over the front of the bag to find the correct position for the stud. Using the second piece of card, fix the stud to the flap through the lining only.

Finishing the Inside of the Bag

Turn the bag to the wrong side. Fold in the front edge, A1–A1, clipping the curves, and press. Hem the pressed edges of the lining over all the raw edges of the gussets and the front edge of the bag, as neatly as possible.

Turn the bag to the right side. Fold down the flap and fasten. Push in the gussets.

Using a cloth, press the bag lightly to re-establish all the folds.

A Semicircular Clutch Bag

The idea for the embroidery on this bag comes from a 1920s cross stitch pattern. The canvas used in this example is a double canvas with 10 pairs of threads to the inch (2.5cm). Should you wish to use a smaller gauge canvas to work a smaller bag, change the diameter of the pattern and length of the zip accordingly.

To work the clutch bag shown on page 40, which measures approximately 5 × 10in (10 × 25cm), you will need the following.

MATERIALS

- 1 piece of double canvas with 10 pairs of threads to the inch (2.5cm), 13 × 13in (33 × 33cm)
- 1 piece of lining material, 11 × 11in (28 × 28cm)
- 9in (23cm) zip fastener
- Approx. 39in (1m) bias binding, 1½in (3.5cm) wide
- 2 skeins each of green DMC stranded cotton Nos. 3346 and 3347
- 1 skein each of DMC stranded cotton: pink Nos. 196, 223 and 3350; yellow Nos. 677, 727 and 3045; and black No. 310
- 60g blue Appleton's crewel wool No. 748
- Sylko sewing thread to make up the bag
- 1 HB pencil
- Adhesive (PVA or Evostik Impact 2)
- Compasses

NEEDLEWORK SKILLS INVOLVED

- Cross stitch
- Straight machine stitching
- Slip stitch

Preparing the Canvas

Mark the centre of your canvas square and, with the compasses, draw a circle with a radius of 5¼in (13.5cm). Draw in a horizontal diameter and two lines parallel to it, one ½in (1.5cm) above and one ½in (1.5cm) below the diameter (see diagram 27).

Put your canvas on a frame as described in Chapter 8.

Working the Embroidery

All the embroidery is worked in cross stitch. Each stitch is worked over one

pair of threads. DMC stranded cotton was used for the flowers, and the background was worked in two strands of Appleton's crewel wool. To find the position to start and the stitch pattern for the flowers, follow the charts in diagrams 28, 29, 30 and 31.

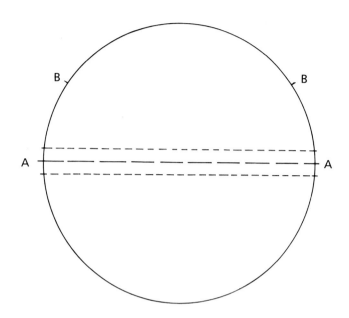

27 *Pattern for semicircular bag*

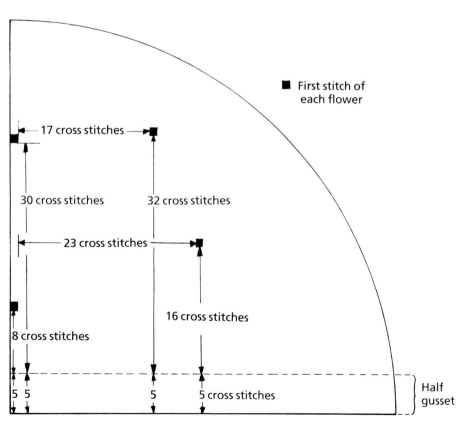

■ First stitch of each flower

17 cross stitches

30 cross stitches   32 cross stitches

23 cross stitches

16 cross stitches

8 cross stitches

5   5   5   5 cross stitches

Half gusset

28 *Positioning the embroidery*

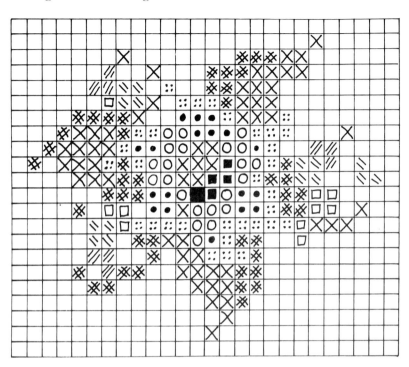

⊠	Light green
⊠	Dark green
∷	Light pink
●	Medium pink
O	Dark pink
▢	Light yellow
╲	Medium yellow
╱╱	Browny yellow
◼	Black
■	First stitch, black

29 *The large flower*

30 *The small flower*

31 *The medium flower*

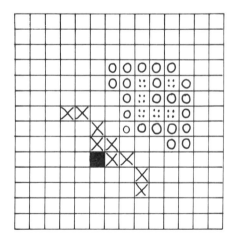

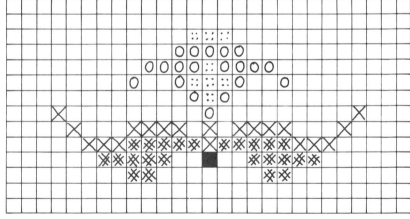

O	Dark pink
∷	Light pink
⊠	Light green
■	First stitch, light green

O	Dark pink	⊠	Dark green
∷	Light pink	■	First stitch, light green
⊠	Light green		

Stretching the Canvas

When the embroidery is finished, take the canvas off the frame. Stretch it upside-down over a damp cloth (as described in Chapter 8), and leave it for several days to dry.

Making Up the Lining

Cut a circle with a diameter of 11in (28cm) from the lining material. Fold the circle in half, and stitch from A to B on both sides (see diagram 27).

Open this seam and press lightly. Now flatten the points and stitch across them, ¾in (2cm) away from the tip (see diagram 32).

Fold both the pointed flaps back to the fold line of the bag lining and catch stitch them to the lining. The lining is now ready to go into the bag.

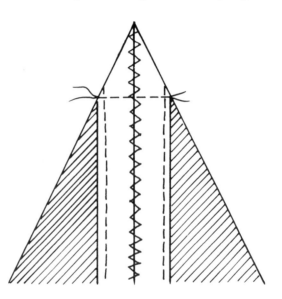

32 *Stitching across the gusset points*

Making Up the Bag

Leaving a seam allowance of ¼in (5mm), cut off the surplus canvas. To keep the cut edge of the rim firm, brush it with adhesive and leave to dry.

Beginning at one of the points A on diagram 27, place the bias strip on the canvas, right sides together and with the raw edges level. It is not necessary to neaten the two ends of the binding, as they will be concealed in the gusset.

Machine ¼in (5mm) from the edge, with the canvas side uppermost, so that you can see exactly where to sew – just where the embroidery finishes.

Turn the bias strip over to the wrong side of the canvas. Press the edge gently, with steam. Tack down the bias binding with small stitches on the front and long ones on the back. These stitches will be hidden by the lining.

The stitches on the front should come out just in the ditch where the bias binding and canvas join. Press the bound edge.

Fold the circle in half, at points A, right sides together. Using a matching thread, slip stitch the bound edges together invisibly and strongly, from A to B on each side (see diagram 27).

Making the Gusset Tucks on the Bag

Flatten out the points at A and stitch across them, ½in (1cm) away from the tip (see diagram 32). Fold the points to the bottom of the bag and catch stitch them to the canvas. Turn the bag through to the right side. Inspect the bag carefully for any gaps in the embroidery along the top edge and around the gusset, and fill in any holes with tent or cross stitches.

Fitting the Zip

Open the zip. Working with one side of the zip, lay the right side of the zipper tape to the wrong side of the bag, along the top edge between B and B. The teeth of the zip should be against the tacking on the bias binding. Back stitch in place by hand. As before, the stitching on the front of the bag should be in the ditch, where the binding and canvas join. Sew in the second side of the zip in the same way.

Making a Tassel

To make opening the zip easier, make a small tassel. Use some of the threads left over from the embroidery and follow the instructions in Chapter 8.

Fitting the Lining

Slip the lining into the bag, wrong sides together. Hem the turnings of the lining opening to the tapes of the zip fastener. Close the zip.

OPPOSITE
Project 7 – an oval shoulder bag for the summer. The white linen is decorated with pulled work, and there is a top zip fastener.

An Oval Linen Shoulder Bag for the Summer

To make the shoulder bag shown on page 45, which measures 6½ × 10½in (16.5 × 26.5cm), you will need the following.

MATERIALS

- 1yd (1m) of evenweave linen with 26 threads to the inch (2.5cm), 36in (90cm) wide
- 1yd (1m) of lightweight, iron-on Vilene
- 18in (46cm) of firm cotton lining, 36in (90cm) wide
- 1 ball of crochet cotton or something similar (the thread size should match one thread of your linen fabric)
- Coats Sylko thread for machine stitching
- Pressing cloth
- 8in (20cm) zip fastener
- 1 tapestry needle No. 24 for working the pulled thread work
- 1 sharp needle for darning threads into the back of the work
- Optional interfacing: 1 piece of thin foam rubber, approx. 6 × 10in (15 × 26cm)

NEEDLEWORK SKILLS INVOLVED

- Simple machine stitching or hand sewing
- Tacking
- Setting in zip
- Pulled thread embroidery
- Overcasting by hand or machine
- Making a buttonholed bar

Cutting Out the Materials

From your evenweave linen cut out the following pieces:

- 1 rectangle for the sides of the bag, 22 × 7½in (56 × 19cm)
- 1 oval piece for the bag bottom, 10¼ × 3½in (26.5 × 9cm)
- 2 half ovals for the bag top, each 2¼ × 10¼in (6 × 26.5cm)
- 2 pieces of fabric for the bag strap, each 50 × 2¼in (127 × 6cm), each with a centre join

From the Vilene and lining cut the same number of pieces as for the linen, except for the bag strap, which is self-lined.

Preparing the Linen

Overcast all the edges of the linen pieces, by hand or machine, to prevent fraying. A seam allowance of ½in (1cm) has been given, except on the bag top centre zip, where it is ⅝in (1.5cm).

Placing the Pulled Work Design

Bring together the two short ends of the linen rectangle to find the centre. Mark the fold from top to bottom with a line of tacking stitches. This identifies the front and back of the bag. Divide each half again in the same way to find the centre front and back lines. Mark these with tacking stitches. You now have a framework on which to build and balance your embroidery pattern.

Our example shows a band, 1¼in (3cm) deep, of honeycomb stitch, patterns of mosaic stitch evenly spaced above it and a sprinkling of eyelets above that. You can use any stitches and patterns you like but make sure to arrange them in a balanced way.

Diagram 33 shows another idea for a border pattern. It was made by cutting up and rearranging a paper square. Added lines give weight to the lower part of the design. Its strong, geometric shapes are very suitable for pulled work.

When the embroidery is complete, press the linen on the wrong side under a damp cloth and with a hot iron.

Making Up the Bag

Fuse the Vilene to the wrong sides of the sides, bottom and tops of the bag. Join the side seam of the bag by hand (see Chapter 8 for backstitch) or machine. Press open the seam.

33 *A simple border pattern, designed by cutting and re-arranging a paper square. Added lines give weight to the lower part of the design. The strong, geometrical character of the pattern makes it suitable for pulled work.*

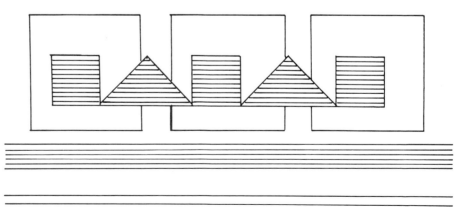

Making Up the Strap

Turn the seam allowances on both the long edges of the two strap pieces to the wrong side and press. Matching the centres, pin the two pieces wrong sides together. Slip stitch the two pieces together. Top stitch the long edges by machine, very close to the edge. Pin the ends over the side seams at the bottom edge of the right side of the bag (see diagram 34).

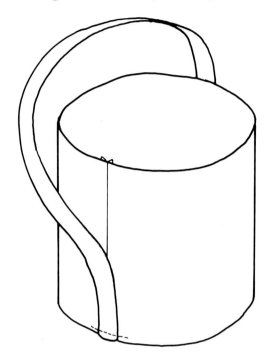

34 *Sewing the strap to the bag*

Inserting the Base of the Bag

With pins, mark the oval base of the bag into quarters as shown in diagram 35. Turn under the seam allowances at the bottom of the bag and the oval base. Matching up the sides and centres with wrong sides together, first pin, then hand stitch the base into the bottom of the bag, easing around the curve of each end (see Chapter 8).

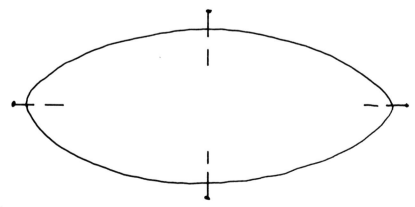

35 *Quartering the oval base*

Fitting in the Top of the Bag and the Zip

Tack the two half ovals, right sides together, down the centre, taking ⅝in (1.5cm) seam allowance. Machine 1¼in (3cm) at each end and press this seam open. Lay the right side of the closed zip under the seam, with the teeth directly under the tacking. Pin in place across the zip. Machine stitch all around the zip, ¼in (5mm) from the centre line, using the zipper foot (see diagram 36).

Take out the tacking and half open the zip. Insert the top in the same way as the base.

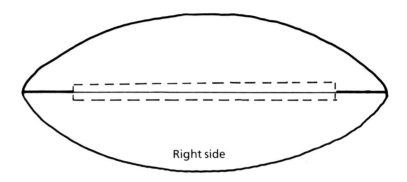

Right side

36 *Stitching in the zip*

Attaching the Shoulder Strap

Open the zip fully. Lay the shoulder strap against the sides of the bag and stitch firmly to the bag, ¼in (5mm) from the top, using a buttonholed bar (see Chapter 8).

Optional Interfacing

Should you wish to stiffen your bag, insert the piece of thin foam at this stage, catching it to the seam allowance. This should be removed when you launder the bag.

Lining

Make up the lining in the same way as the bag, omitting the zip, but preparing the opening by turning under the seam allowance and pressing it. You could put an optional pocket into the lining before sewing up the side seam.

Push the lining into the bag, wrong sides together, and hem the pressed opening edges over the zipper tapes at the top. Turn the bag right side out.

Tassel

Make a small tassel of linen threads to attach to the zip pull (see Chapter 8 for making tassels).

Practical Bags for Everyday Use

THERE is no reason why embroidery should be used exclusively on bags for special occasions. Many techniques are suitable for sturdy, practical, everyday bags, without being too pretty or elaborate. For example, simple machine embroidery, counted thread work, patchwork and canvaswork can look smart and sophisticated. Before designing your day bag consider carefully what it will have to hold, from the car keys to a personal organizer. Nothing is more maddening than trying to remove a cheque book from a bag that is too small for it – although it may prevent you from spending any money! Put together all the items you usually carry around with you when you are away from home for a day and design your

LEFT
A practical denim bag for everyday use. The colourful, bold design is applied by machine with straight stitching only.

OPPOSITE
Bags for everyday use. Left: *a canvaswork bag with leather trimming;* right: *a canvaswork shoulder bag with leather trimming; and* below: *a semicircular clutch bag made of wool fabric, padded and decorated with leather.*

day bag around them. Consider its size and whether you prefer to carry it over your shoulder or in your hand. Do you need inner pockets? If so, remember that these usually have to be stitched into the lining before it is made up.

A day bag needs to be more robust than an evening bag, and it will probably need more stiffening and stronger fastenings, straps and handles. For ideas on style and fashion keep an eye on up-market magazines and scan the more expensive leather goods and shoe shops for up-to-date trends. Don't be afraid of using leather. Once you have got used to handling it and taking the trouble to use the correct interfacing, adhesives, needles and machine foot, the end result will look satisfyingly professional. Before working on a leather skin, spray it well with a proprietary protector to prevent little marks spoiling it while you work. Keep washing your hands, especially if you are using adhesive. This will also help to avoid grease marks which seem to appear from nowhere, just where you don't want them.

When you have made your first successful day bag, you will doubtless begin to think of more challenging projects to tackle, and you will certainly find yourself looking harder at bags that you admire. Try to work out how they are made, why they work well and how you can adapt the idea for yourself.

Before you start work on a bag style that is new to you, make a mock up. The fabrics you use may be remnants, but their character should be similar to the fabrics you plan to use for the actual bag – that is, use soft remnants if the bag is to be a soft, floppy one, or stiffer materials for the mock up of a firmer bag.

The mock up should be cut and sewn exactly as the bag proper. It should have all style details, such as piping or gathers, although, of course, there is no need for any embroidery. Zips and other fasteners and handles need only be tacked into position. Once you have taken the trouble to go through every stage of the making up process with your mock up, you will feel confident and relaxed when it comes to cutting and sewing your embroidered bag. When you have spent hours embroidering a piece of fabric, you don't want to spoil it.

An Easy Pattern for a Stylish, Adaptable Bag

On the following pages we describe how to make a mock up for an unusual design, which lends itself to most embroidery techniques, from patchwork to canvaswork to free machine embroidery. By attaching different kinds of handles to suit different fabrics and decorations the character of the bag can be changed from sporty to elegant.

The size of the bag depends on the width of the handle. So first of all, chose your handle (see diagram 37). The overall shape may be kept the same or it may be varied slightly, but the method of making up will remain the same. The handle of the large bag on page 54 is made of brass (see suppliers list). It is attached to the bag by two prongs. The frame is approximately 9in (23cm) wide and the prongs are 5in (12.5cm) apart. As the style favours a stiff fabric, we chose calico for our practice piece.

To work the calico mock up on page 54, which measures 9in (23cm) across the top fold, you will need the following.

MATERIALS

- **Paper to make up pattern**
- **1 handle with a span of approximately 9in (23cm)**
- **1 piece of calico, 2yd (2m) of 36in (90cm) width fabric or 1¼yd (1m) with careful cutting of 60in (1.4m) width fabric**
- **Medium iron-on Vilene, 9in (23cm)**
- **3yd (3m) piping cord**
- **Sewing thread**

NEEDLEWORK SKILLS INVOLVED

- **Straight machining**
- **Piping**
- **Tacking**
- **Hemming**

Making the Paper Pattern

The pattern in diagram 38 is for a handle with a span or opening of 9in (23cm). If your chosen handle is a different size, you must adjust the pattern accordingly, but you should keep the same proportions.

Using your pattern paper, enlarge the pattern in diagram 38 to fit your handle. Add ½in (1cm) seam allowance around the outside and to the

Project 8 – at the back is a calico mock up for an elegant day bag with a dual-purpose metal handle, which is available commercially. In front is a smaller variation of the same bag, but this has an easy to make wooden support and a hand-knotted shoulder strap.

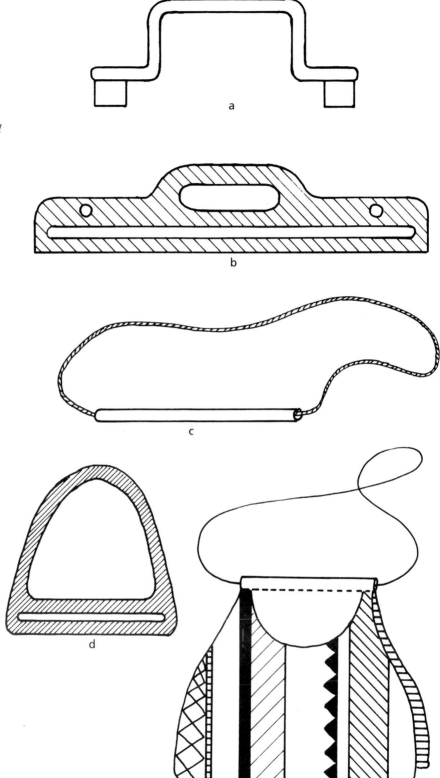

37 *Some of the handles that can be used on day bags.* **(a)** *A commercially produced brass handle, of the kind used on page 54. The prongs on each clamp simply require firm pressure in a vice. Remember to protect the brass.* **(b)** *and* **(d)** *Handles of this type are readily available in needlework and craft shops. The finished bag need only be pushed through the space provided, and the two pouches of the bag machined or stab stitched together beneath the handle.* **(c)** *A metal tube is stitched into the top fold of the bag by machine (use the piping foot) and a strong cord or strap is passed through it.* **(e)** *A cord is fixed through holes in each end of a flat piece of wood, which is then stitched into the top fold of the bag, using the piping foot.*

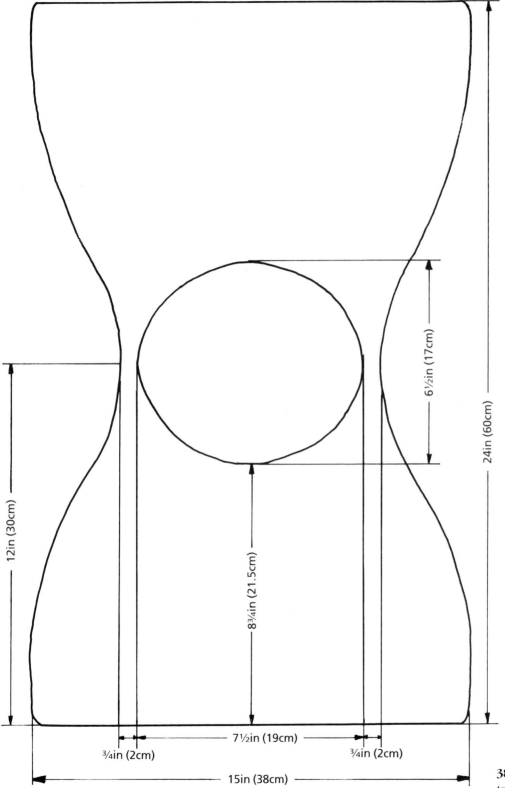

24in (60cm)

6½in (17cm)

12in (30cm)

8¾in (21.5cm)

7½in (19cm)

¾in (2cm)

¾in (2cm)

15in (38cm)

38 *Basic pattern for enlarging to fit a handle 9in (23cm) wide.*

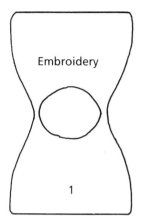 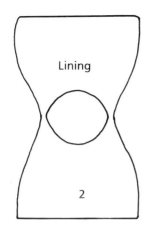 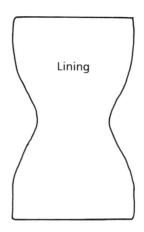 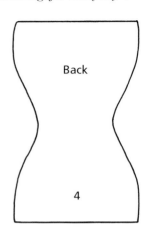

39 *The four sections needed to make up the large bag on page 51.*

central opening. Use your paper pattern to cut out two shapes from your fabric with central holes and two without holes (see diagram 39).

Piping the Central Opening on Piece 1

Prepare the piping as described in Chapter 8. Tack the piping to the central opening of piece 1, within 1in (2.5cm) either side of the joining point. Join the two ends of piping neatly in the following way:

1 Cut one end of the piped cord at the desired meeting point.
2 Unpick and peel back some of the bias fabric from the other end of the piping.
3 Cut off the exposed cord at the meeting point (see diagram 40).
4 Fold under the raw edge of the loose bias, wrap it around the opposite piece of piping and tack it in place (see diagram 41).
5 Machine around the opening, using the zipper/piping foot.

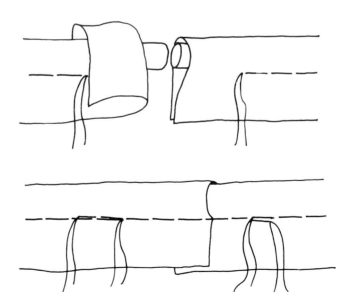

40 *Join the piping – the trimmed piping is on the right, and the exposed and trimmed cord is on the left*

41 *The bias strip on the left is turned under and wrapped over the piping on the right*

Facing the Outer Bag (Piece 1)

Pin and tack pieces 1 and 2, right sides together, and machine around the central opening, over the stitch line of the piping, clipping the seam allowance at frequent intervals up to the stitch line. Turn the facing through the opening to the wrong side and press. Tack all the outer edges together.

Piping the Edge of the Bag

Attach the piping to the edge of the bag, joining the ends neatly as described above.

Stiffening

Cut a piece of Vilene to fit across the central saddle area of piece 3 (see diagram 39), and fuse it to the wrong side of the lining.

Finishing the Bag

Place piece 3 on a table, right side up. Lay the joined pieces 1 and 2 on top, with the intended embroidered side uppermost and with all raw edges level. Place piece 4 on top, wrong side uppermost. Pin and tack in place. Beginning at one of the two bottom edges, machine round the bag following the previous stitch lines, leaving an opening of 3–4in (7–10cm). Clip the curves and trim the corners of the seam allowance. Turn the bag to the right side, through the bottom opening. Press and close the opening with hand stitching.

Handles

Attach your chosen handle (see diagram 37).

A Practical Day Bag

To make the shoulder bag shown on page 62, which measures 15 × 11in (30 × 41cm), you will need the following.

MATERIALS

- 18in (50cm) of linen furnishing crash, 54in (1.4m) wide
- 2 pieces of heavy taffeta lining, each measuring 12 × 16in (30 × 41cm)
- 1 piece of leather, approx. 8 × 12in (20 × 30cm)
- 2 pieces of leather, each ¾in (2cm) wide and 21in (53cm) long
- 16in (40cm) zip fastener
- 10in (25cm) zip fastener
- 2 D-rings to take a ¾in (2cm) wide strap
- 2 pieces of lightweight iron-on Vilene, each measuring 12 × 16in (30 × 41cm)
- 2 pieces of lightweight iron-on Vilene, each measuring ¾ × 21in (2 × 53cm)
- 2 pieces of lightweight iron-on Vilene, each measuring 8 × 12in (20 × 30cm)
- 4 stud fasteners
- Marker pen
- 1 piece of card, 3 × 3in (7.5 × 7.5cm)
- Glue stick (Pritt Stick)
- Adhesive (Evostik Impact 2)
- Stitch and Tear

NEEDLEWORK SKILLS INVOLVED

- Straight machine stitching
- Backstitch, by hand or machine
- Fitting a zip

Preparing and Cutting the Leather

First apply the iron-on Vilene pieces to the wrong side of the appropriate pieces of leather, using a damp cloth and only a medium hot iron. If your iron is too hot the leather will shrink. Then cut from your piece of leather measuring 8 × 12in (20 × 30cm) the trimmings shown in diagram 42.

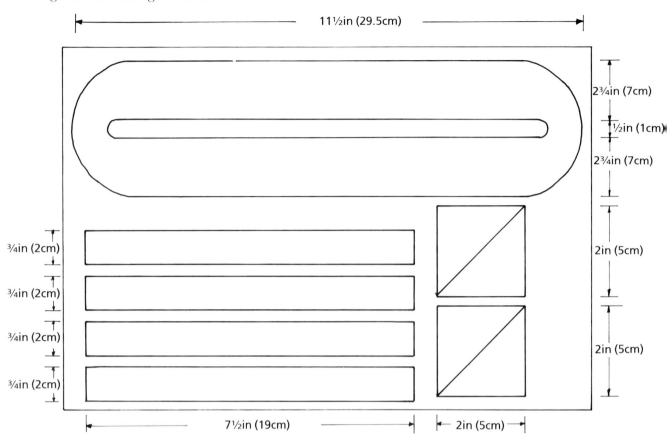

42 *Lay out pattern for the leather trimmings*

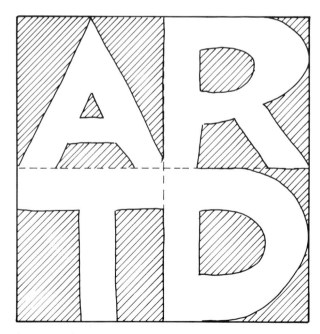

43 *Logo design*

Cutting the Material

From the crash, cut the following:
- 2 rectangles, each measuring 12 × 16in (30 × 41cm) for the front and the back of the bag
- 1 rectangle, 12 × 13in (30 × 33cm)
- 1 strip, 4 × 36in (10 × 90cm) for the shoulder strap

Designing the Logo

Arrange your chosen lettering in a square 3 × 3in (7.5 × 7.5cm) in any way you find pleasing, but making sure that the letters fill the square well. Stick this design on to the card and cut it out with scissors or a craft knife to make a template (see diagram 43).

Applying Your Logo to the Bag Front

On the rectangle of crash for the front of the bag, mark the stitching line ½in (1cm) from all edges, including the zip trim area. Beginning in one corner of the marked out space, place your logo template on to the crash and draw around it. Cover the whole space with your logo in this fashion, creating a rhythmical pattern (see diagram 44).

Working the Embroidery

Stitch the design by machine, as shown in the photograph, or by hand if you prefer, using pearl thread (coton perlé) and backstitch (see Chapter 8 for backstitch).

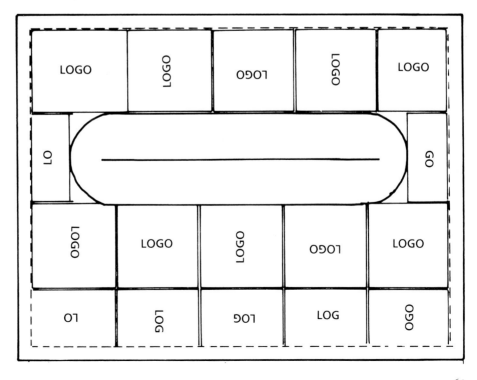

44 *Placing the design on the fabric*

Making Up the Bag

INTERFACING

Apply the appropriate pieces of Vilene to the wrong side of the front and back pieces of the bag, again using a damp cloth to iron.

FRONT POCKET ZIP

Slash, turn under and stick down the seam allowances on the pocket opening in the front of the bag (see diagram 45).

Pin the 10in (25cm) zip under the neatened opening and, using the zipper foot, machine it in place with straight stitching. Keep the zip closed.

Stick the leather trim over the zip opening. Top stitch using the leather foot and needle.

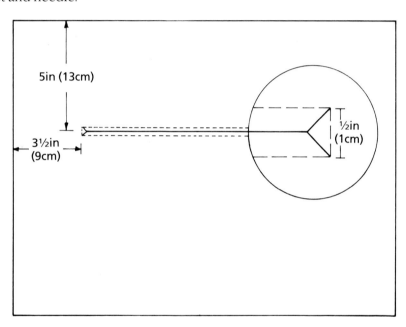

5in (13cm)

3½in (9cm)

½in (1cm)

45 *Slashing the front in preparation for inserting the zipper*

POCKET

Stitch one edge of the pocket piece to the lower zip tape. Fold the pocket piece down and press as shown in diagram 46. Use a pressing cloth to protect the zip.

Bring the bottom edge of the pocket piece level with the upper zip tape. Stitch the pocket edge to the zip tape (see diagram 47). Stitch all remaining open pocket edges together, at the top and down the sides.

TOP ZIP

On the front of the bag, lay the closed zip to the top edge of the bag, right sides together. Stitch along the stitch line, close to the teeth, using the zipper foot.

Apply the zip to the back of the bag in exactly the same way, keeping the side edges level. Open the top zip. Machine the sides and base of the bag in one long seam, taking ½in (1cm) seam allowance. This should guide you around the edge of the embroidered area on the front of the bag. Trim the corners, turn and press into shape.

GUSSET POINTS
Flatten out the points at the two bottom corners of the bag. Stitch across the points, 1½in (4cm) from the tip (compare this with diagram 32).

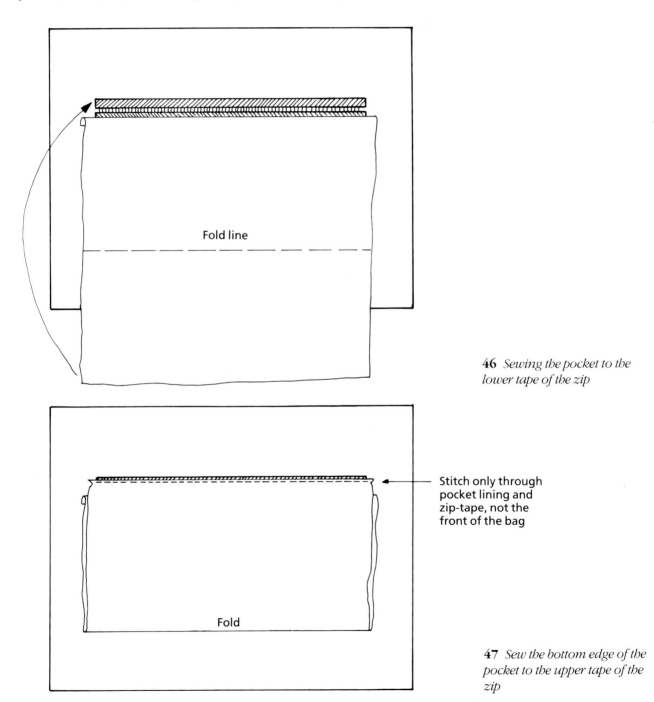

Fold line

46 *Sewing the pocket to the lower tape of the zip*

Stitch only through pocket lining and zip-tape, not the front of the bag

Fold

47 *Sew the bottom edge of the pocket to the upper tape of the zip*

Making Up the Shoulder Strap

Fold the strap in half lengthwise and machine it, taking ½in (1cm) seam allowance. Press the seam open and turn the strap through to the right side. Turn in each end and slip stitch together to neaten. Press the strap into shape.

Preparing the Trim

Thread each one of the long leather trims through a D-ring and enclose it in a 3in (8cm) long loop. Stick the last inch (2.5cm) of the loop to the wrong side of the trim (see diagram 48).

Applying the Trim to the Shoulder Strap

Machine the fabric ends of the shoulder strap over the side seam of the bag, about ½in (1cm) down from the top of the bag. To make it strong, stitch a square over the strap end (see diagram 48).

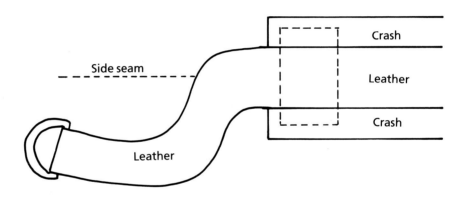

48 *Attaching the D-rings to the strap*

Making Up the Gusset Straps

With your four gusset strips, make two pairs and stick them, wrong sides together, to form two straps. Cut one end of each strap into a point. Put some Stitch and Tear under the straps, and top stitch all sides close to the edges. Enclose each gusset point of the bag in two triangular leather trim pieces. Insert the flat end of the gusset strap into the point of this sandwich and top stitch through all layers, again using Stitch and Tear.

Thread the pointed ends of the gusset straps through the D-rings of the shoulder straps. Adjust them for length and punch in the stud fasteners in the appropriate places.

Drawstring Bags

JUDGING by the popularity of drawstring bags, they must be favourites with all embroiderers. The reason may be that their construction is so simple and requires only tools and techniques that are familiar to all needlewomen; it may be their versatility, since they can be seen, small and elegant, in the bridesmaid's hands at the altar, as well as large and practical, at the side of the sports track.

Their character can be changed simply by using different materials, while the basic construction stays the same. The drawstring closure is so 'textile friendly', that it is easily adapted to many styles or made part of the decoration of a bag. Look at diagram 49 and imagine a row of fine eyelets worked around the top of a small silk bag and, threaded through them, a thin, hand-twisted cord with a tassel at either side, and you will see in your mind's eye an evening bag. Now look at the same illustration, imagine it large and made of calico, with a rope as drawstring with a knot at the end, and you will see a sports bag or sailor's kit bag.

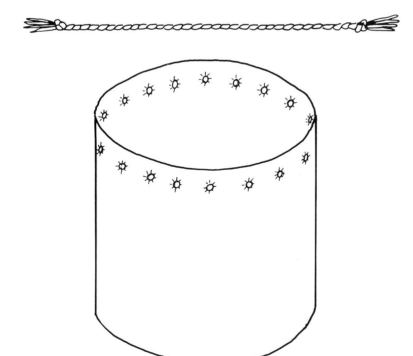

49 *A basic drawstring bag*

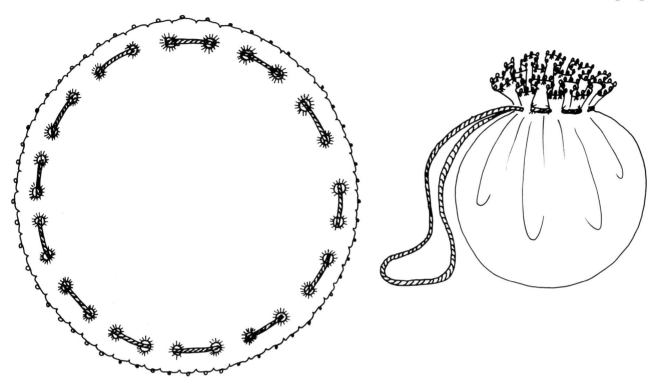

50 *A simple style of drawstring bag*

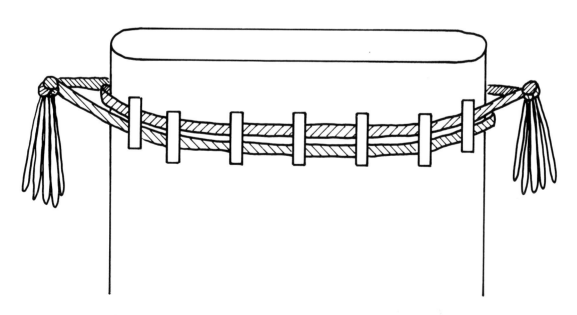

51 *How to arrange two drawstrings*

The simplest pattern for a drawstring bag is a circle of fabric with a number of holes around its circumference, through which a string or cord is threaded (see diagram 50). This draws up into a pouch, ready to be filled with anything, apart from small coins, which are more safely kept in a purse (see Chapter 1).

Another pattern that is suitable for drawstring bags but that is more economical with the material is made up of two parts: a base, sometimes stiffened, and an attached fabric tube, which is cut on the straight (see page 76). If two drawstrings are used, as shown in diagram 51, it is easier to open and close the bag. The strings may be threaded through a channel, as in project 10, a dolly bag, or in and out of rings on the outside of the bag as in project 14, a sports bag. They may go through rings or loops attached to the inside or the outside of the bag, and you may use metal rings or rings you have made from threads (see Chapter 8). For hand-twisted cords see Chapter 8.

Only a few styles of drawstring bags have been mentioned here. With some imagination you will create many more, also making use of other needlework techniques, such as crochet, macramé and lacemaking.

OPPOSITE
Three drawstring evening bags. Top: lurex fabric was covered with circular patterns made from knitted tubular yarn pulled into small petals and stitched down, and then embroidered in straight stitch using two strands of Anchor stranded cotton and embellished with small beads; right: hand-dyed silk was decorated with parallel rows of running stitch in silk thread and with a handmade, beaded fringe, while the drawstring of hand-twisted silk is finished off with large acorn shapes covered with detached buttonhole stitch; and below: black cotton poplin was decorated with small pieces of brightly coloured silk, held down with a zigzag machine stitch, worked using a metallic thread.

52 *A dolly bag from Turkey, with a well-arranged border. This bag is firm and has a stiff neck; smocking would give the same effect.*

A Dolly Bag

To make a dolly bag, suitable for use as a work bag, you will need the following.

MATERIALS

- 1 piece of fabric, 26 × 26in (66 × 66cm)
- 2 circular pieces of fabric, diameter 10in (25cm)
- 2 circular pieces of stiff card, diameter 8in (20cm)
- 1 cord, approx. 56in (1.4m) long
- Sewing cotton
- 2 wooden beads
- Adhesive (Evostick Impact 2)
- Bodkin or small safety pin to thread cord

NEEDLEWORK SKILLS INVOLVED

- Straight machine stitching
- Making a simple buttonhole
- Embroidery technique of your choice – for example, cross stitch, automatic machine stitching, appliqué or patchwork

Placing and Working the Embroidery

The most suitable area to embroider is the circumference of the bag, near the base, where it will be seen to its best advantage. Place your design along one side of your fabric, about 1in (2.5cm) from the raw edge.

Work your embroidery along the whole length of the fabric, up to 4in (10cm) deep. Leave ½in (1cm) seam allowance at the beginning and the end of the border (see diagram 53).

Pockets

On the opposite side of the fabric to the embroidery, fold under 6in (15cm), and, with wrong sides together, press and machine 4in (10cm) from the folded edge, forming a 4in (10cm) wide tuck (see diagram 54).

Fold this towards the embroidery and press. Then machine stitch as shown in diagram 55 to form six pockets.

Making Up the Bag

Place the two, now shorter sides of the oblong, right sides together and

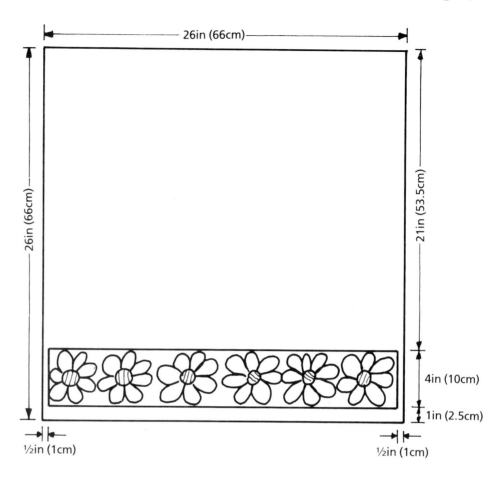

26in (66cm)

26in (66cm)

21in (53.5cm)

4in (10cm)

1in (2.5cm)

½in (1cm)

½in (1cm)

53 *Placing your design on the bag*

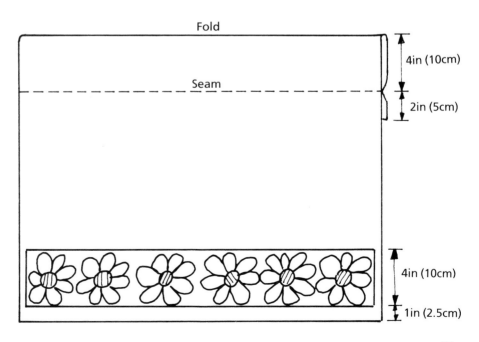

Fold

Seam

4in (10cm)

2in (5cm)

4in (10cm)

1in (2.5cm)

54 *Making the tuck*

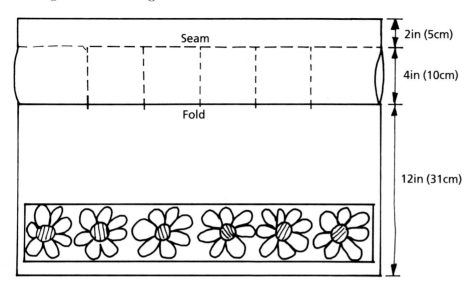

55 *Stitching the pockets*

machine, taking ½in (1cm) seam allowance. Press the seam open. Fold this tube in half, wrong sides together, and with the embroidery on the outside and the pockets on the inside. Make sure the pockets open the right way up.

Press the folded edge, and tack the two raw edges together, taking ½in (1cm) seam allowance.

Channel for Drawstring

Machine all the way around the bag, ½in (1cm) from the folded edge.

Work two small buttonholes directly underneath the machine stitching and into the outer fabric only, one into the side seam and the other opposite the side seam.

Machine a second time around the bag, this time ½in (1cm) below the first seam and just below the buttonholes. This forms the channel for the drawstrings of the bag (see diagram 56).

Fitting the Base of the Bag

Turn the bag inside out; the pockets are now on the outside. Divide the circumference of the bag into quarters by folding it twice and marking with pins.

Divide the circumference of the fabric circles into quarters, also by folding twice and marking with pins. Pin one of the circles to the bottom edge of the bag, right sides together and matching the quarter marks. Ease the fullness of the circle equally around the base of the bag. Machine all the way round carefully to avoid puckers, taking ½in (1cm) seam allowance and stitching on the tacking line. Insert one of the circular pieces of card. Press the seam allowance over the edge of the card towards the centre of the circle and glue on to the card.

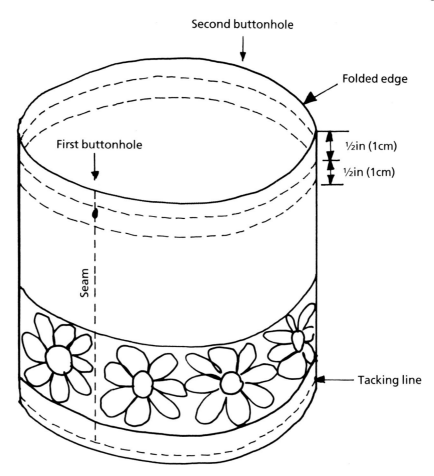

Second buttonhole

Folded edge

First buttonhole

½in (1cm)

½in (1cm)

Seam

Tacking line

56 *Making the drawstring channel*

Lining and Stiffening the Base of the Bag

Place the other piece of card on the second fabric circle. Press and stick the seam allowance over the edge of the card. Lay this circle on to the stiffened base of the bag, wrong sides together. Oversew by hand or stick down. Turn the bag right side out.

Adding the Drawstring

Cut the length of cord in half. Thread one half through the buttonhole in the side seam, guide it through the channel, all the way around the bag, and out again by the side seam. Thread both ends of this cord through one of the beads and tie a knot, about 1in (2.5cm) from the ends of the cord. Fray the ends.

Thread the second piece of cord in the same way, but starting and finishing at the opposite buttonhole. Attach the bead, and knot and fray the end of the cord as before. If you pull on the beads in opposite directions, the dolly bag should close easily.

A Smocked Linen Bag

To make the linen bag shown on page 76 you will need the following.

MATERIALS

- 1 piece of linen with approx. 24 threads to the inch (2.5cm), 25 × 13in (63.5 × 33 cm)
- 3 shades of cotton or linen embroidery thread, 2 skeins dark, 1 skein each of medium and light
- Sylko sewing thread
- 1 disc of card, diameter 2½in (6cm)
- 2 circles of linen, diameter 4in (10cm)
- 1 circle of iron-on Vilene, diameter 4in (10cm)
- Emery board
- 1 tapestry needle No. 24 for pulled work
- Sewing needle for smocking

NEEDLEWORK SKILLS INVOLVED

- Simple smocking
- Making a buttonholed ring
- Making a cord
- Making a tassle
- Squared edging pulled fabric stitch
- Pulled work eyelets

Preparing the Fabric

Overcast the edges of the linen by hand or machine to prevent fraying.

Gathering

Put seven rows of gathers along one long side of your linen rectangle by picking up two threads of linen every six threads. The rows should work out exactly the same, each pair of picked up threads being the same warp threads of the linen (see diagram 57).

Smocking

Leaving a ½in (1cm) seam allowance at each end of the embroidery, work the smocking from the top as follows.

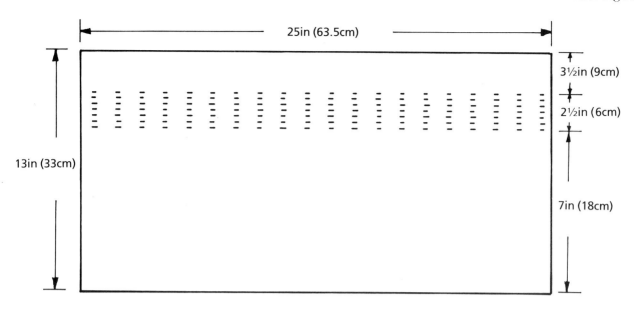

25in (63.5cm)

3½in (9cm)

2½in (6cm)

13in (33cm)

7in (18cm)

57 Pattern for the smocked bag and gathering guide

Row 1 Cable stitch, worked in the darkest colour just above the first line of gathering.

Row 2 The same as row 1, but worked just below the first line of gathering.

Row 3 Stem stitch (sometimes called outline stitch), worked in the lightest colour just above the second line of gathering. The thread has been held below the needle.

Row 4 The same as row 3, but this time worked just below the second line of gathering and with the thread held above the needle.

Row 5 Trellis stitch worked in the darkest colour over ten pleats. The top of each point is worked just below the previous row of smocking, and the bottom of each point is worked just below the third line of gathering.

Rows 6 and 7 Trellis stitch worked in the medium shade. Each row is worked just below the one above.

Row 8 A fourth row of trellis stitch, this time worked in the darkest colour. The bottom of each point should be worked just above the fourth line of gathering.

Rows 9 and 10 These should be worked just below the fourth line of gathering, in the lightest colour, exactly the same as rows 3 and 4, but this time hold the thread above the needle on the first row, and below the needle on the second row.

Row 11 Trellis stitch worked in the darkest colour over twelve pleats. The top of each point should be worked just above the fifth line of gathering. The bottom of each point should be worked just above the sixth line of gathering.

Rows 12 and 13 Trellis stitch worked in the medium colour. Each row should be worked just below the one above.

Row 14 A fourth row of trellis stitch, this time worked in the darkest colour. The bottom of each point should be worked just above the seventh line of gathering.

Steaming the Embroidery

Lay the embroidery face down on the ironing board, cover it with a damp cloth and hold a hot iron over the work, without pressing at all.

Closing the Side Seam

Join the side seam, aligning the ends of the smocking exactly. It is important that the 3½in (9cm) of the seam above the embroidery are accurately joined. You may prefer to do the whole seam by hand.

Press open the seam without squashing the smocking.

Working the Top Edge with Squared Edging Stitch

Begin to work this edge 1¼in (3cm) away from the top row of smocking stitches. Hold the bag sideways and travel from the top downwards (see diagram 58). Work over four threads. The edge is worked in two stages. Follow diagrams 96 and 97 in Chapter 8.

Work two rows of four-sided stitch to give a firm yet delicate-looking finish.

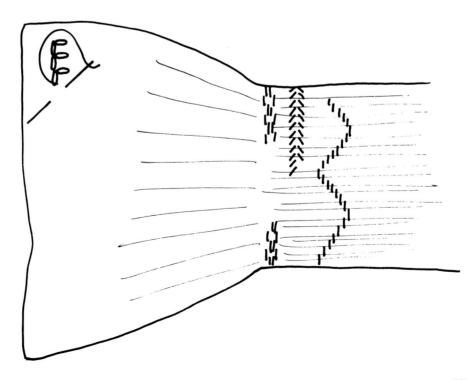

58 *How to hold the bag for working the squared edging stitch*

Working the Eyelets

Work some eyelets in a random way over the lower part of the linen (see Chapter 8). Make larger eyelets over six or seven threads below smaller ones worked over three or four threads.

Press the work on the wrong side under a damp cloth.

Sewing in the Base

Having cut out the disc of card, buff the edges with an emery board to smooth them. Cover it with iron-on Vilene. Run a gathering thread around one of the linen circles and pull it tightly the Vilene-covered card. Fasten off firmly.

Gather or pleat finely the bottom edge of the bag. Draw up the bottom to fit under the linen-covered disc, with a turning of ½in (1cm). Pin the disc over the bottom edge and stitch in by hand with a decorative herringbone stitch (see Chapter 8).

Turn under ½in (1cm) on the second circle of linen and press. Turn the bag inside out and pin the second circle over the first, covering the raw edge. Hem the circle into place.

Drawstring and Rings

Make six buttonholed rings (as shown in Chapter 8) and pin them evenly around the inside of the bag. Sew them to the pleats of the smock gathers just above the first row of smocking. Make a twisted cord and thread it through the rings (see Chapter 8).

Finish each end of the cord with a tassel (see Chapter 8).

Evening Bags

AT TIMES, while we were researching for this book, it seemed that evening bags are the only ones considered suitable for embroidery. We hope that by now you realize that this is not true. However, this is the area in which the embroiderer really can allow her or his imaginative powers to work overtime and explore more fully some of the showy and dramatic techniques, which are really suitable only for dressy occasions. Metal thread techniques are among those that immediately suggest themselves for evening use, and a small bag is not too ambitious a project for such a time-consuming and expensive method.

Delicate fabrics, such as silks, nets, lace and beaded textiles, and three-dimensional decoration, which would not withstand daily wear, can be used. Several methods may be combined to produce an extra rich surface – quilting with machine embroidery and fabric painting, insertion stitches with machine embroidery, smocking with beading or pulled work, to name but a few techniques. Patchwork does not have to be rustic looking and traditional. Worked in silks or other rich materials, such as lurex or even gold kid, it can be elegant and sophisticated. Flowers, leaves, tassels, rouleaux, fringes and stump work can all play their part in creating very exciting and beautiful work.

When you are designing and making an evening bag, it is still important to plan and finish off the job properly, paying attention to stiffenings, fastenings and carrying straps or handles. Don't let your enthusiam for the embroidery allow you to neglect these very important details. Remember how much more flattering it is for someone to ask: 'You didn't make that, did you?' rather than, 'Did you make it yourself?'

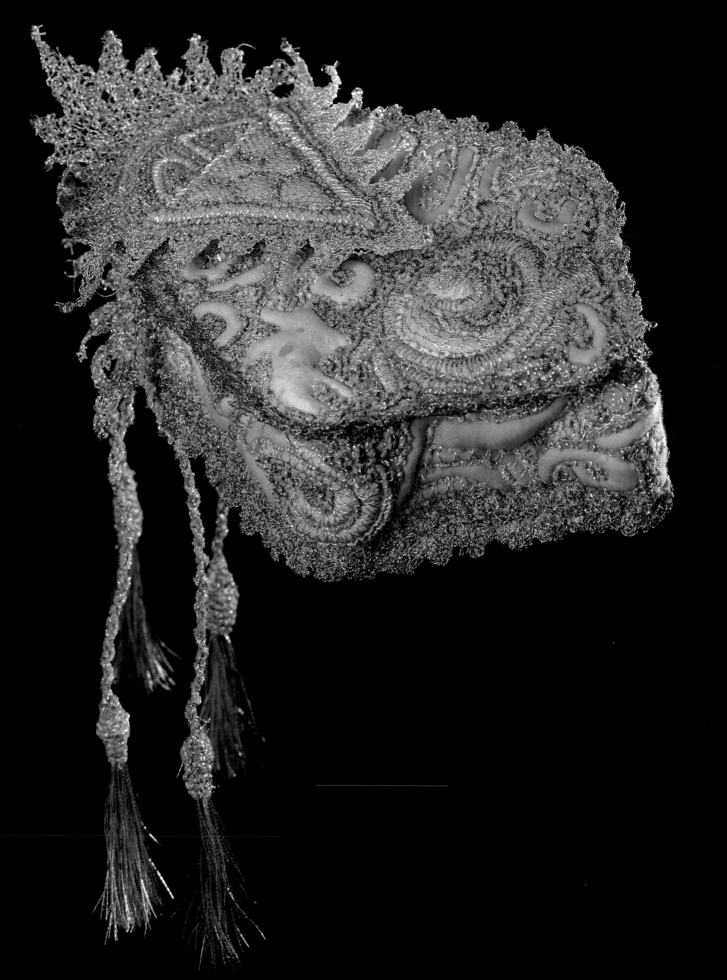

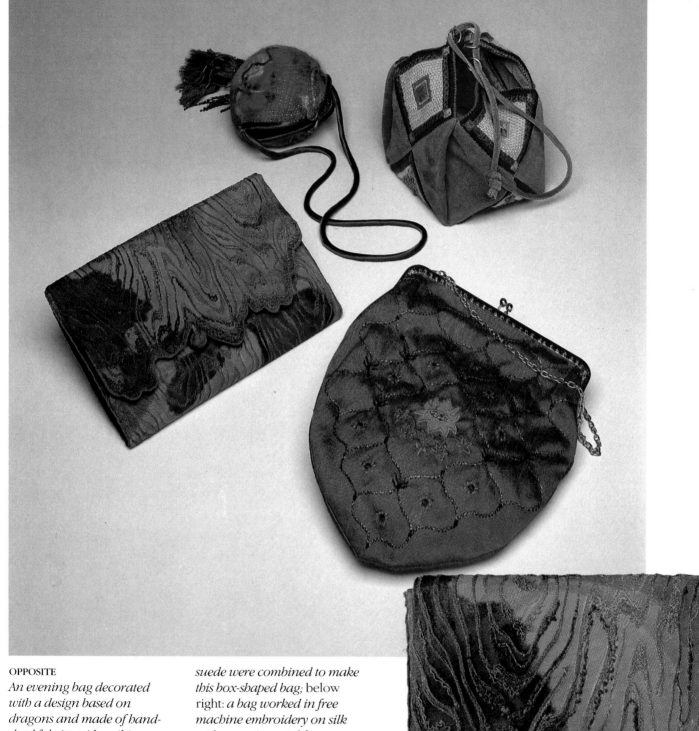

OPPOSITE
An evening bag decorated with a design based on dragons and made of hand-dyed fabrics with quilting, machine embroidery and lace.

ABOVE
Evening bags made in a variety of techniques. Top left: *handmade felt was moulded over a tennis ball to make this satin-trimmed and beaded bag;* top right: *canvaswork and suede were combined to make this box-shaped bag;* below right: *a bag worked in free machine embroidery on silk with a sew-in metal frame;* below left: *free machining emphasizes the design of the fabric used to make this clutch bag.*

RIGHT
A detail of the clutch bag shown above.

A Small Shoulder Bag

To make a shoulder bag in the style of the one shown on page 85, which measures 7 × 7in (18 × 18cm), you will need the following.

MATERIALS

- 9in (25cm) of silk, 36in (90cm) wide
- 9in (25cm) of lining fabric
- 1 piece of heavy sew-in Vilene, 20 × 8in (51 × 20cm)
- 1 piece of thin foam for extra interfacing, 20 × 8in (51 × 20cm)
- 1yd (90cm) of chain or cord for shoulder strap
- 2yd (1.8m) of fine string or piping cord
- Adhesive (Evostik Impact 2)
- 1 button mould
- Sewing thread for making up

NEEDLEWORK SKILLS INVOLVED

- Simple machining
- Tailor's tacks
- Oversewing
- Hemming
- Applying piping
- Making a rouleau loop with covered button

Decorate your fabric in any way you like; see pages 80, 81 and 85 for some suggestions.

Making a Paper Pattern

Make a paper pattern following diagram 59. Note that no seam allowance is given on the pattern.

Cutting and Preparing the Fabrics

Cut out the silk, adding a seam allowance of ½in (1cm). Mark all the points given in the diagram with tailor's tacks. Cut out the Vilene exactly the same size as the silk. Tack the silk to the Vilene around the edge.

Piping

Apply piping to the flap edge, tapering it away into the seam allowance at points A–A. Apply piping to the front D–D (see Chapter 8 for piping).

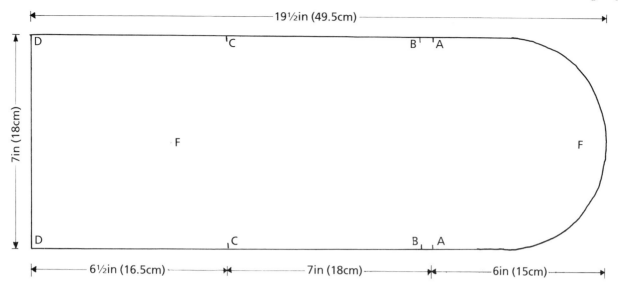

19½in (49.5cm)

7in (18cm)

D   C   B   A

D   C   B   A

6½in (16.5cm)   7in (18cm)   6in (15cm)

59 *Pattern for the silk evening bag*

Applying the Rouleau Loop

Make a 1½in (4cm) length of rouleau, as narrow as possible (see Chapter 8 for making rouleaux).

Bend it in half and stitch it in place as shown in diagram 60.

The Flap

Cut out the lining fabric exactly the same size as the bag. Place the flap ends of the bag and lining fabric right sides together and stitch around the flap from A to A, stitching on top of the piping seam.

Trim away the Vilene close to the stitching, and reduce the seam allowance to ¼in (5mm).

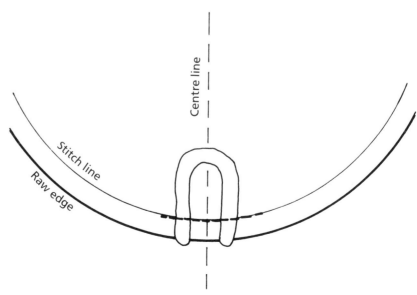

Centre line

Stitch line

Raw edge

60 *Applying the rouleau loop*

Side Seams and Gussets

Keeping the flap and the bag lining out of the way, fold the bag at C, right sides together. Machine stitch up to B. At the corner C, snip the seam fold up to the stitching (see diagram 61).

Press open the side seam. Flatten the corner at C and stitch across ½in (1cm) away from the tip, to form a gusset (see diagram 62).

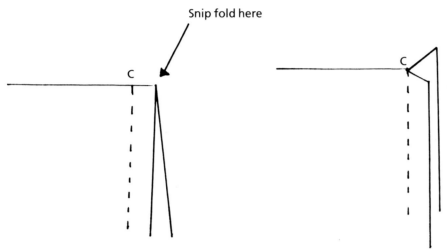

Snip fold here

61 *Snipping the corner to open the seam*

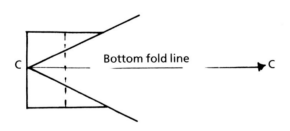

Bottom fold line

62 *Stitching across a gusset point*

Interfacing

Cut a rectangle of thin foam to fit the front of the bag, without turnings. Spread a very thin coating of adhesive on the foam and stick it carefully to the Vilene interfacing on the bag front. Trim the remaining piece of foam to fit the back and the flap, and stick this in the same way on to the remaining sections of the bag.

Leave this to dry thoroughly, weighing the foam down lightly with a magazine or thin book. Do not press too hard or the adhesive may penetrate the Vilene and stain the silk. When it is completely dry, turn the bag through to the right side.

OPPOSITE
Evening bags. Top left: *project 12 – a small silk shoulder bag, decorated with patchwork and with machine-embroidered, three-dimensional leaves and flowers;* right: *a bag made of fabric that was roller-printed with metallic dyes before being worked in Somerset patchwork;* and below: *the design for this goldwork bag was developed from a simple doodle and worked on black wool crêpe, the front being embroidered with gold threads and beads while the back of the bag is machine-quilted with gold silk threads.*

Lining the Bag

Fold the lining at C, right sides together, and stitch up the side seams to within ½in (1cm) of point B. Make a gusset at point C, in the same way as you did on the bag (see diagram 62).

Push the lining into the bag. Turn under the remaining seam allowances on both the bag and the lining and oversew them together very neatly at each side. The lining should be invisibly hemmed close to the piping along the front edge.

Cover a button with silk according to the manufacturer's instructions, and stitch it to the front of the bag.

Finishing

Close the bag and press it gently, under a pressing cloth. Neatly sew either a thin chain or a cord at each side, under the flap.

A Silk and Canvaswork Bag in White and Cream

To make the bag shown on page 89, which measures 12in (30cm) square, you will need the following.

MATERIALS

- 1 square of lightweight calico, 13 × 13in (33 × 33cm)
- 2 squares of habutai silk or similar fabric, each measuring 13 × 13in (33 × 33cm)
- 1 bias strip of habutai silk, 1½in (3cm) wide by 20in (50cm) long
- 1 piece of interlock (non-fray) single embroidery canvas with 14 threads to the inch (2.5cm), 18 × 11in (45 × 27.5cm)
- 4 pieces of polyester wadding, each measuring 6 × 3in (15 × 7.5cm)
- Coats pearl cotton (coton perlé) No.5
- Sewing thread to make up the bag
- 1yd (1m) of thick piping cord
- 1 packet of seed pearl beads (approx. 80 beads)
- 12 larger pearl beads
- 1 water-soluble marker pen

NEEDLEWORK SKILLS INVOLVED

- Canvas embroidery
- Zigzag satin stitch by machine
- Making a piped rouleau

Preparing the Canvas

Mark the canvas using the measurements given in diagram 63. Mark the centre of each square, and put the canvas on a slate frame as described in Chapter 8.

Working the Embroidery

Beginning in the centres, cover each square with a pattern of canvaswork stitches of your own choice, using the pearl cotton. The bag shown on page 89 was embroidered in a variety of satin stitches and tent stitch. A change of texture was achieved by altering the direction of the stitches, so that the light catches the sheen of the thread at different angles. In addition, some stitches were raised by padding or tramming them with a long couched

thread (see Chapter 8). Work within two threads of your marked squares. When the embroidery is complete, stretch it as described in Chapter 8. Cut the canvas to separate each square, trimming away the canvas to your marked line.

Applying the Canvas to the Bag

Mark the calico into 16 squares by folding it accurately, pressing and tacking through the fold lines. Find the exact centre of your calico square (see diagram 64). Place one of the silk squares onto the calico square and pin as shown in diagram 65. Match the centre of the large embroidered square with the centre of the calico/silk square, and pin or tack it in place.

With some spare canvas, silk and calico, practise machine satin stitching to find the correct density of stitches to apply your embroidery. Stitch on the central square. Pin and stitch the four small squares to the silk/calico, removing any pins from beneath the small squares as you reach them. The corners of the small squares should just touch those of the large square and all the squares must be perfectly straight.

OPPOSITE

Evening bags. Top: *project 13 – a canvaswork and silk bag (see also above);* centre: *the design is based on fish scales and was worked with silk, stranded cotton, wool and metallic threads in* petit point, *and the cords are hand knotted;* below: *a smocked silk bag with beading.*

ABOVE

Project 13 – a silk and canvaswork bag in white and cream, decorated with a few beads.

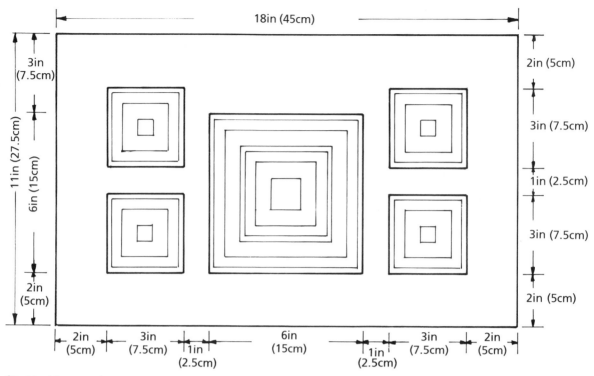

63 *Marking out the squares on the canvas*

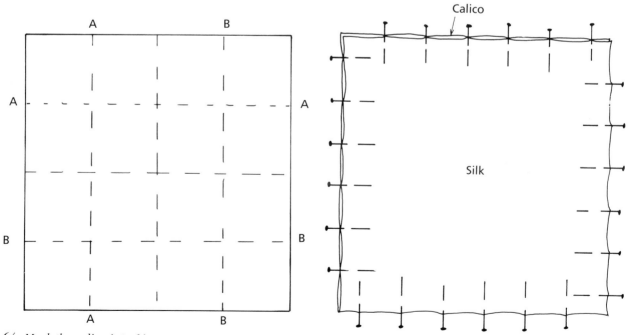

64 *Mark the calico into 16 squares, fold it accurately and press*

65 *Pinning the silk to the calico*

Quilting

Remove all the remaining pins. Slip a rectangle of wadding between the calico and the silk on each side of the square, smoothing it out with your fingers inside the sandwich. Pin together the open sides. Sew a scattering of small seed pearls on to the silk at intervals, stitching through all the layers of the fabric. This will give a quilted texture.

The Strap

Make 20in (50cm) of corded rouleau as described in Chapter 8. Cut off 18in (46cm), and machine stitch one end of the piped rouleau to the seam allowance of each of two adjacent corners. Stitch the short piece of rouleau to the opposite two corners (see diagram 66).

The Lining

Mark points A and B on the silk lining and join A to B on all four sides (see diagram 64).

Making Up the Bag

Using the machine, join A to B, right sides together, on all four sides. Catch stitch each resulting point to its nearest corner of the large canvas square.

Turn under and press the seam allowances on the bag and the lining. Turn the bag right side out, and sew a large pearl to each point of the canvas squares. Push the lining into the bag, wrong sides together, and hem the edge to the edge of the bag. To close, pull the large rouleau loop through the small one.

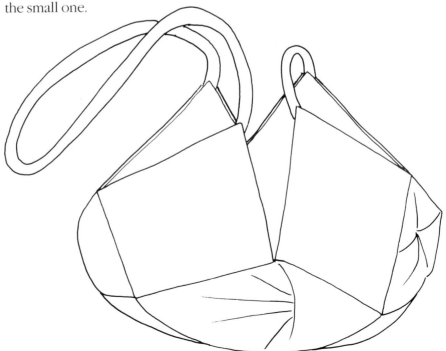

66 *Placing the rouleau strap*

Work, Sports and Shopping Bags

WHY do so many of us carry our belongings around in unattractive plastic carrier bags? Instead of being mobile advertisements for our local supermarkets, would it not be more satisfactory to advertise our own skills and ingenuity and create exciting and amusing containers for our possessions?

In this chapter you will find some ideas for making larger bags for holding your sports gear, needlework and daily shopping. For some of these a quick technique is more suitable than anything too elaborate, so you will find ideas for machine embroidery and quilting. Fabric paints are another interesting possibility, as they are easy and cheap, and quick and effective to use.

Bags can be made waterproof by lining them with shower curtain plastic. You may need to support these with Stitch and Tear while you are machining. You may also find the leather foot (silicon coated) better for stitching. Plastic has been used to line the sports bag on page 92. It would also be a good lining for a bag to contain anything a baby needs for a day out. Some commercially made baby bags even have a zipped compartment at the bottom to house a potty, but this may be a bit ambitious, even for the most devoted granny to contemplate. The larger areas of these bags makes them ideal for some of the bolder techniques, such as appliqué and patchwork.

With one or two successful special purpose bags to your credit, you could find yourself with several requests from family and friends to make something jolly and personal for them – so be warned.

OPPOSITE
Sports bags. Top right: *a beach bag made of dyed cotton with transfer-dyed umbrellas and machine appliqué;* left: *project 14 – a spray-dyed calico sports bag decorated with hand and machine embroidery;* below right: *a sports bag decorated with machine appliqué and free machine stitching.*

A Sports Bag

To make the sports bag shown on page 92, measuring 19 × 18in
(48 × 46cm), you will need the following.

MATERIALS

- 1 piece of firm calico, washed and ironed, 39 × 22½in (100 × 57cm)
- 2 pieces of calico, each measuring 7 × 13½in (17 × 36cm)
- 1 piece of plastic shower curtain fabric, 17 × 39in (43 × 100cm)
- 1 piece of plastic shower curtain fabric, 7 × 13½in (17 × 36cm)
- 1 strip of iron-on Vilene, 3½ × 39in (9 × 100cm)
- 1 strip of polyester wadding, 10 × 39in (25 × 100cm)
- 1 piece of cotton lawn, 10 × 39in (25 × 100cm)
- 1 reel Coats machine embroidery thread
- Coats Anchor stranded embroidery cotton in a few bright colours of
  your choice
- 1 piece of firm card, 6 × 12½in (15 × 32.5cm)
- 58in (1.5m) of thick piping cord
- 16 brass rings, large enough for the piping cord
- 1 large brass swivel trigger clasp or dog clip
- 1 tambour frame, minimum diameter 12in (30cm)
- 1 sheet of dressmaker's carbon paper
- Blotting paper
- Tracing or greaseproof paper
- 1 ballpoint pen
- Fabric paint, blue (Deka)
- 1 diffuser

SKILLS INVOLVED

- Spray painting
- Tracing
- Quilting
- Long and short stitch
- Machine sewing
- Tacking

Spraying on the Design

Should this technique be new to you, practise on scrap paper before you
begin to work with your fabric. Work outside if it is a fine day or protect
your work table and floor with plenty of old newspapers.

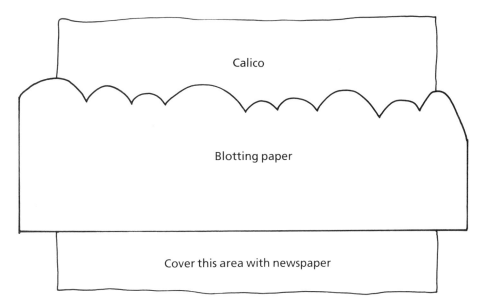

Calico

Blotting paper

Cover this area with newspaper

67 *Preparing the wave template for spraying*

Place the washed and ironed piece of calico that measures 39 × 22½in (100 × 57cm) on the table with one of the long sides towards you.

Cut an inverted wave pattern into one of the long sides of the blotting paper and lay it on top of the calico, with the wavy side 2in (5cm) from the top edge. Only these 2in (5cm) should be exposed, the rest of the fabric should be covered by the blotting paper and additional newspaper (see diagram 67).

Pour the dye into a deep, narrow flask or glass; it may need diluting. Stick the diffuser as deep into the dye as possible. Now blow steadily into the diffuser, spraying an even, thin layer of blue dye over the exposed calico.

Carefully lift the blotting paper and replace it 1½in (4cm) closer to you. Again, spray evenly over the calico. The area sprayed first will now get its second coat of dye.

Repeat this three more times, or until 12in (30cm) of the fabric are covered with waves.

Fix the dye by ironing the back of the calico with a hot iron for up to 10 minutes, or as the dye manufacturer recommends.

The Swimmers

Trace the two swimming figures and the diver from diagrams 68, 69 and 70, using tracing or greaseproof paper.

Arrange the figures on the waves as you like. You may turn them upside down or back to front and repeat them as often as you like. Try to bring variety into your arrangement.

Place some dressmaker's carbon paper, shiny side down, between the tracing paper and the painted calico. Now go over your drawing with a ballpoint pen to transfer the figures to the calico.

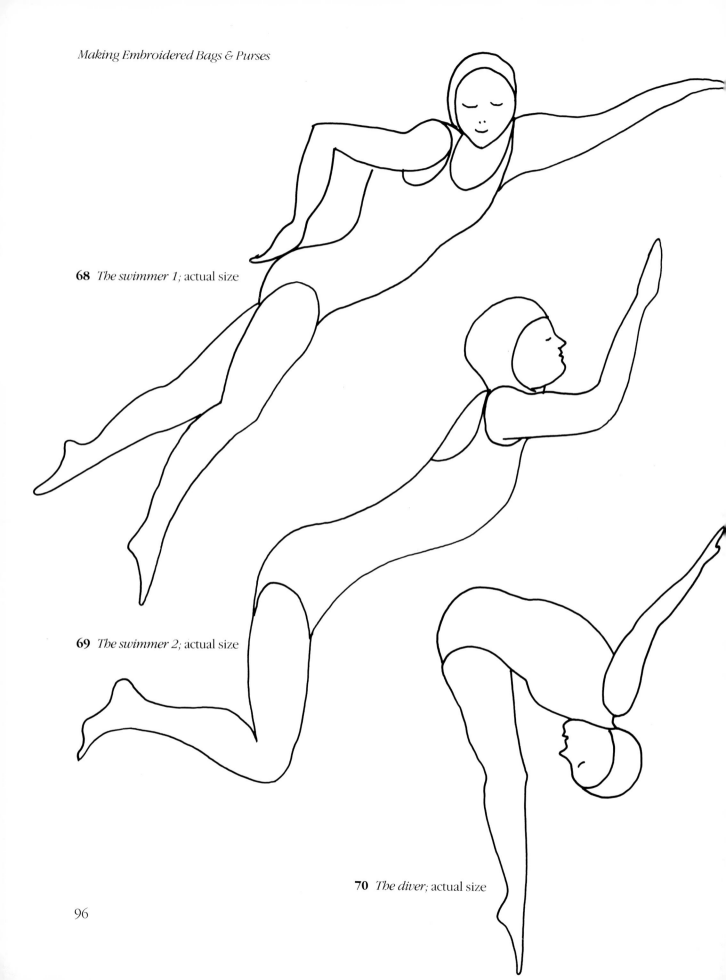

68 *The swimmer 1; actual size*

69 *The swimmer 2; actual size*

70 *The diver; actual size*

Quilting

Place the calico, face down, on the table. Cover the back of the waves first with the polyester wadding, then with the cotton lawn. Tack this sandwich together with several rows of large stitches. Quilt the wave shapes, avoiding the figures, either by hand with backstitch, or by machine with the feed lowered and the darning foot attached.

Now quilt the swimmers in the same way.

After all the quilting is completed, trim away the surplus wadding and lawn from the back of the work, above the level of the top wave.

Embroidering the Figures

Use a 12in (30cm) tambour frame to hold your work while you embroider. A frame with a table clamp is best, as it leaves both hands free to stitch. Choose some bright colours for the swimwear and cover it with long and short stitch.

BELOW
A detail of the sports bag, project 14, showing the spray-dyed waves with stitched outlines and a swimmer (see also page 92).

Thread your needle with one strand of the stranded cotton, make a knot in the end and enter the fabric from the right side, a little way away from the neck line and work a few tiny running stitches along the outline to secure the thread. The first row of straight stitches is worked over the outline. The subsequent rows should come up and split the previous row, to give a smooth, satin appearance (see Chapter 8).

Making Up the Bag

Fuse the strip of Vilene along the upper edge of the bag. With a ½in (1cm) seam allowance, join the plastic lining to the calico, right sides together. Do not press – the plastic will melt when it is touched with a hot iron. Join the seam of the bag, calico and plastic lining, in one long seam, with a 1in (2.5cm) seam allowance. Use Stitch and Tear under the plastic section.

Fold the lining to the inside of the bag, with the lower edges level. At the bottom edge, hold the plastic and calico together with a row of wide zigzag stitches.

Attaching the Bottom Loop

Make a loop from 6in (15cm) of the cord. Splay out the ends and place it over the seam on the right side of the bag. Machine several times over the ends, ½in (1cm) from the edge (see diagram 71).

Base

Measuring to the right, mark a point A, 6½in (17cm) from the seam, and, again, mark a point B, 12½in (32cm) from the seam. Repeat these, again

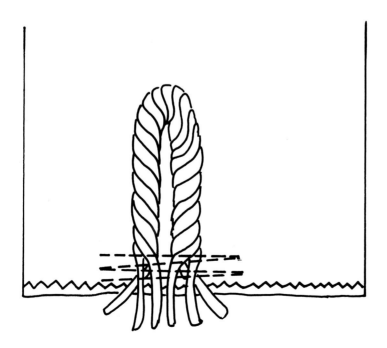

71 *Attaching the cord loop*

measuring from the seam but this time to the left. Match the four corners of the base of the bag with these points and, taking ½in (1cm) seam allowance, sew the base in place.

Cover the piece of card with the rectangle of plastic using a suitable adhesive. Turn the bag right side out and glue the stiffened inner base into the inside bottom of the bag, covering the seam allowance.

Drawstring and Rings

On the outside, place 16 brass rings evenly around the top of the bag, 2in (5cm) below the edge, and sew them on firmly. Thread the remaining cord through the rings, starting and finishing near the seam. Thread the cord through the ring of the brass trigger swivel and splice or knot the ends together.

Additional Techniques

Dressing a Slate Frame for Hand Embroidery

♦

The most useful frame to support canvas for hand embroidery is a slate frame. Basically it consists of four pieces of wood. Two of these have webbing attached to them, and they are called rollers or rails. They will, in some way, be connected to the two other plain pieces of wood, which are called stretchers, and thus form a square or a rectangle in which your canvas will be suspended (see diagram 72).

It is important that your canvas is framed up on the straight of the grain, without any distortion. To achieve this, proceed as follows.

1 Bind the side edges of your canvas with tape or masking tape to prevent damage to the canvas and to stop your yarns catching on the bristly edges of the canvas.
2 Mark the centre of the canvas.
3 Measure the length of the rollers and mark the exact centre points of the rollers on the webbing with indelible ink.
4 Match the centre points of the canvas with those on the webbing. Pin the canvas in place on to the webbing. Start at the centre of the top roller, sew to one side and again, starting from the centre, sew to the other side.

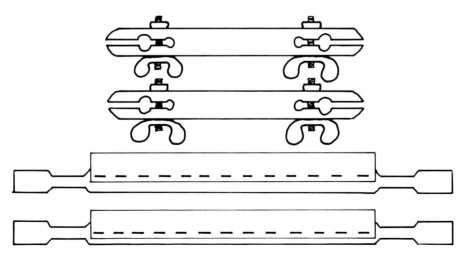

72 *Parts of a slate frame*

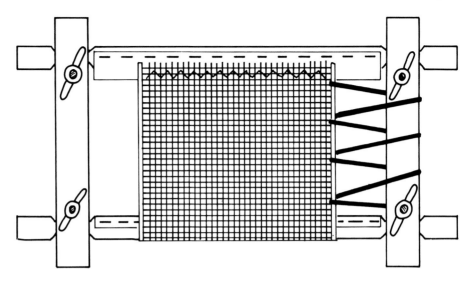

73 *The dressed frame*

Attach the bottom edge of the canvas to the other roller in the same way. Take care not to use the second roller back to front.

5 Now, according to the construction of your frame, fix the stretchers to the rollers.

6 Your canvas will be longer than the stretchers, so you will have to turn the rollers to take up the slack of the canvas until it is taut.

7 Clamp the rollers tight so that they cannot unwind again.

If you are using a new, firm and straight canvas and your piece is not too wide, the above seven steps may be all you have to do to keep your canvas from distorting while you work on it. Otherwise you will have to stretch your canvas not only vertically but also horizontally as follows.

Use a thin string or tape and, beginning at one corner, wind it around the stretcher, then thread it through the bound edge of the canvas and back again around the stretcher. Continue in this way until you reach the bottom end of the canvas (see diagram 73). Lace up the opposite side in the same way. Adjust the tension and fasten off the string or tape ends. This lacing will have to be undone every time you want to unroll new canvas from the rollers.

If your canvas piece is too short to fit into your frame, but you would prefer to work it framed up rather than in your hand, you just sew a piece of straight, strong fabric (calico, for example) on to the webbing of the rollers. If you do this, you must be especially careful about finding the centre points of the canvas, fabric and webbing.

In general, embroidery that has been worked in a frame will look neater. It is also faster to stitch, since you have two hands available to manipulate the needle.

Stretching Your Embroidered Canvas

◆

All canvas work should be stretched after it has been finished and before you start making it up into a bag. If it has been worked in the hand it will look crumpled, but even if it has been worked on a frame and looks superficially tidy, the fibres of the yarn (especially if you have used wool) will be disarranged from their journey through the canvas. They need moisture to get back into order.

Take a rectangular piece of wood, plywood or hardboard, with straight edges and true right angles and larger than your embroidery. Cover it with a damp, soft towel. Keep the towel in place with a few drawing pins. Now lay your embroidery on the towel, right side down. Line up one straight side of the canvas with one straight side of the wood and hold it in place with many stainless steel drawing pins. As you press in the pins pull the canvas in a straight line and parallel to the edge of the wood as hard as you can and the canvas will allow.

Next, stretch a side at right angles to the first one. Pull and pin it, making sure that it also will be parallel to the edge of your board. Now pin down the side opposite the first one, starting in the centre and working towards one of the corners. Pull the canvas tight and keep the edge straight. Finish with the fourth side in the same way. Use as many drawing pins as you can fit in a row. The more you use, the less the strain will be on each individual pin and the less the danger of the canvas tearing out (see diagram 74).

Leave your embroidery in a horizontal position until it is absolutely dry and stiff again. This may take a week or even longer. Let it dry slowly, away from direct heat. Do not cover it with polythene, or your embroidery may go mouldy.

When the towel and the embroidery are completely dry, take out the drawing pins. When you turn your embroidery over to the right side you will be surprised how good it looks. Now it is ready to be made up into your chosen project.

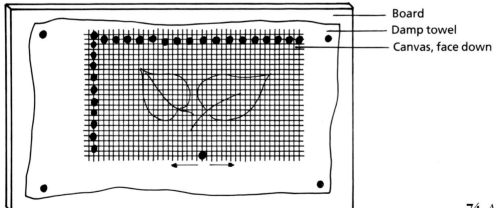

Board
Damp towel
Canvas, face down

74 *A canvas being stretched*

Making a Twisted Cord

◆

You can make a twisted cord from almost any yarn, unless it is very elastic or fragile. Wool will give you a fluffy, soft and light cord. Cotton yarns make up into a strong, smooth cord, which will be quite hard and very durable but is also likely to be stiff. Silk yarn will always twist into a beautiful, very strong cord, with a warm sheen, and it will hang well. Man-made yarns vary such a lot that it is impossible to describe them in a general way. A cord usually has the same character as the yarns from which it is made, and if your man-made yarn is soft and heavy, it will make up into a soft and heavy cord. If you find that your cord is harder than you expected, given the qualities of the yarns you used, it is possible that you overtwisted the cord.

It is possible to be very creative in cord making. Yarns can be mixed, not only yarns of different fibres and colours, but also of different weights. Even fine ribbons, narrow strips of fabric, rouleaux, metal threads and leather thongs can be included in a cord. For the cord used on the butterfly neck purse on page 21 we used 4½yd (5m) of cotton pearl (coton perlé) No. 8, two strands each of light red, dark red, light green and black.

To make a twisted cord, take the yarns of your choice and tie a knot in each end. Loop one end over a door handle or hook and the other over a pencil, dividing the strands into two sets of four. Twist the pencil in a clockwise direction, until the threads snarl up on each other when the tension is slackened (see diagram 75). Hook a weight or a large coat-hanger on to the twisted threads. Lay the weight on the floor and bring the pencil end back to the door handle, with the weight still trailing on the floor to keep the strands taut and prevent them snarling up in an uncontrolled

75 *The four stages in making a twisted cord*

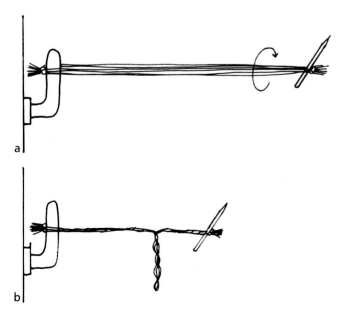
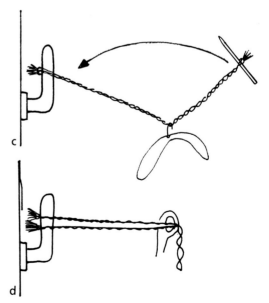

manner. Hook the pencil end of the yarns over the door handle as well. Unhook the weight and, starting from this end, release the twisted strands little by little – about 6in (15cm) at a time – and watch them twist into a cord. Work your way towards the door handle. When all the yarn is twisted, give your cord a good tug before taking it off the door handle. Hold your cord by one end and let the other hang free. You will find it untwists a little. Do not worry, it is only undoing the overtwist and will stop when it has become stable. Tie a knot in the open end.

The cord used for the purse illustrated on page 21 is double twisted as follows. Twist the cord you have just made for a second time in the same fashion as before, only this time turn the pencil in an anti-clockwise direction. Double the cord as before. This is easy now, because it is shorter. Allow it to twist in small steps, give it a good tug and take it off the door handle. Tie a knot in the open end, and unwind the overtwist, should there be any.

You will now have about 1yd (1m) of very strong, colourful cord, with an even, double twist.

Making a Machined Cord

A cord of a variety of sizes and textures can be made quickly on the sewing machine.

Choose whatever threads you want and simply work the zigzag stitch over them. It helps to twist the threads together as you stitch. You will need to experiment with a variety of yarns and also with the degree of swing required.

Cutting a Continuous Bias Strip

Long lengths of bias can be made from quite small squares of cloth. Cut a square diagonally into two triangles. Join the triangles as shown in diagram 76. The joins are all made on the straight grain of the fabric. Point B is marked at the width of the desired bias strip.

Form the strip into a tube by matching A to B and stitching a seam. Note that the points are not level.

Begin to cut the bias at point A–B, and continue until you reach the end.

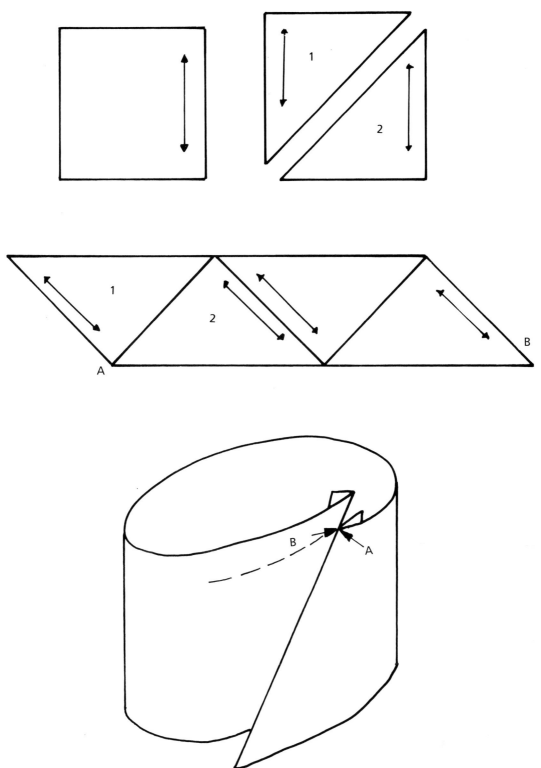

76 *How to cut and join fabric
to make a continuous bias strip*

Making Rouleaux

◆

Cut a strip of bias fabric. Fold it in half lengthwise with the right sides together.

The width of the bias will depend on the type of fabric and size of rouleau you require. Machine down the whole length of the folded bias. The stitch tension should not be too tight. If necessary, trim away a little of the seam allowance, although it is usually better to leave it as a filler for the rouleaux. Turn the length of rouleau through to the right side, using a bodkin and strong thread or a proprietary rouleau turner (see diagram 77).

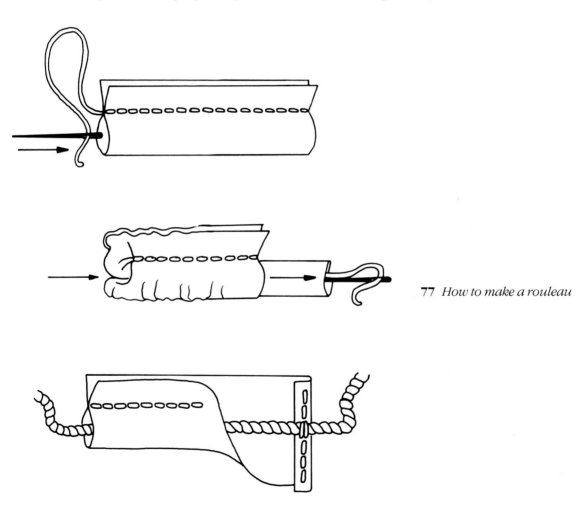

77 *How to make a rouleau*

78 *How to make a piped rouleau*

Making Piped Rouleaux

You need a length of bias strip as long as the rouleau you want to make and twice this length of piping cord. The bias must be wide enough to cover your cord, plus seam allowances. Firmly stitch one end of the bias strip to the middle of the piping cord. Fold the right side of the fabric over the cord and machine stitch, using a zipper foot. Trim the seam allowances. Pull the enclosed cord out of the tube, thus turning the rouleau right side out. Cut off the surplus cord (see diagram 78).

Making and Applying Piping

Cut a length of bias fabric, wide enough to cover your piping cord plus seam allowances. Fit the zipper foot to the sewing machine. Fold the bias strip around the piping cord, wrong sides together, and stitch the length of piping as close to the cord as possible. To apply the piping to a seam, lay it to the right side of your fabric, with the seam allowances level. Pin them together, with the pins at right angles to the seam line. (Note: if you are using leather, do not pin, but glue into place with a suitable adhesive.)

Still using the zipper foot, machine the piping in position. Your stitching should be on the stitch line of the seam. When the piped edge is joined to a facing, lining or to another piece of the bag, the stitching must be done with the zipper foot and on the same line. If you stitch with the piped edge uppermost, you will be able to see exactly where to sew. Snip curves where necessary (see diagram 79).

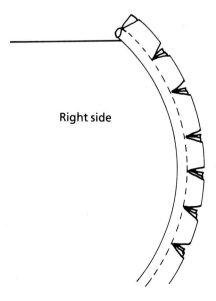

Right side

79 *How to apply piping cord*

Making a Tassel with a Decorated Head

Cut a piece of card as wide as your tassel will be long, including the head of the tassel. Wind your thread around the card until it is sufficiently thick and plump to be attractive. With a length of thread, make a loop and push this under the bunch of threads on the card. Thread the two spare ends through the loop and draw it tight. Slip the bunch of threads off the card.

Thread the two loose ends through a small wooden bead. Draw the bunch of threads back over the bead, distributing them evenly.

Use the two loop threads to tie the tassel neck very tightly, just under the bead. Thread the two ends back through the bead and use them to attach the tassel later. Cut the tassel open and trim the ends. Work detached buttonhole stitch over the head of the tassel, starting at the top, covering the whole head and drawing it into the neck (see diagram 80).

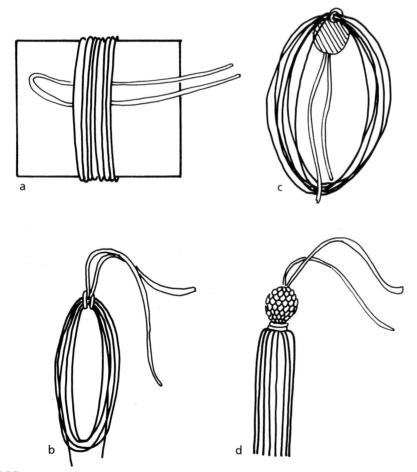

80 *The four stages in making a decorated tassel*

Making a Buttonholed Bar

Lay a foundation of about six threads, going to and fro between A and B. Work buttonhole stitches over them, with the stitches lying close together (see diagram 81).

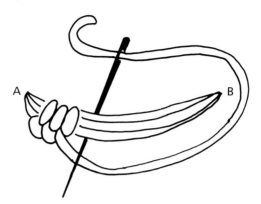

81 *Making a buttonholed bar*

Making a Buttonholed Ring

Wrap a strong cotton or silk thread five or six times around a pencil or a piece of dowelling, according to the size of the rings you need for your cords. Take the loops off the pencil and work buttonhole stitches over the ring of threads to hold them together and to strengthen them. Make sure the ends are made fast with the buttonhole stitches, or use them to sew the rings in place (see diagram 82).

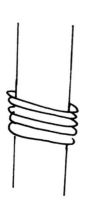

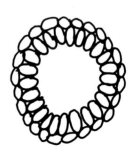

82 *Making a buttonholed ring*

Stitch Diagrams

◆

83 Backstitch
Worked from right to left, the stitches should touch each other.

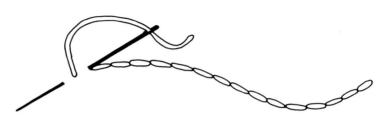

84 Cable stitch *(smocking)*

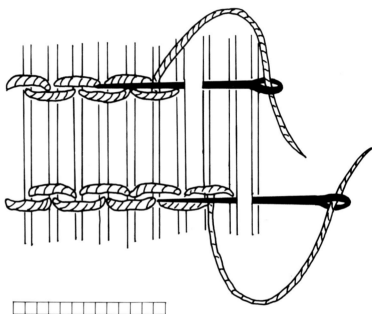

85 Cross stitch
Work the stitch evenly and with the crossing thread always lying at the same angle.

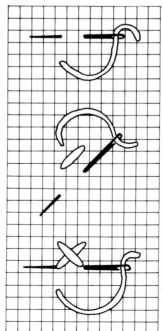

Detached buttonhole
stitch *(see diagram 81)*
This is a simple looped stitch worked over one or more suspended threads.

86 Eyelet *(pulled work)*
Work over different numbers of threads to obtain larger or smaller eyelets. Take care to arrange the last few stitches smoothly

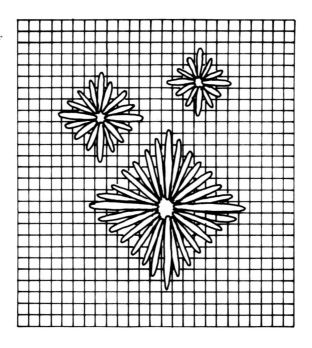

87 Four-sided stitch
(pulled work)
When used together with squared edge stitch (see diagrams 96 and 97) four-sided stitch makes an attractive, strong border with a delicate appearance.

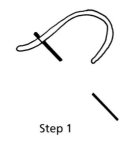

Step 1

Step 2

Step 3

Step 4

Finished stitches

88 French knots
It is important to hold the thread taut while you are twisting it around the needle. Turn the needle around and re-enter the fabric where it first came out. Release the tension only when the knot almost rests on the fabric. The diagram here shows the thread twisted only once around the needle to make very delicate knots. For bolder stitches, wrap the threads around the needle several times.

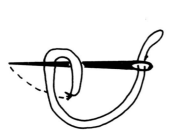

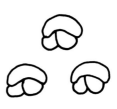

89 Hemming, hem stitch
Work small, neat stitches, not too tightly.

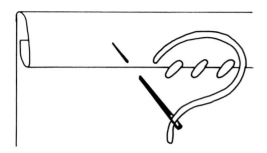

90 Herringbone stitch
This stitch is worked from left to right, but the needle always points to the left.

91 Honeycomb stitch
(pulled work)
A delicate, all over pattern, giving a light texture.

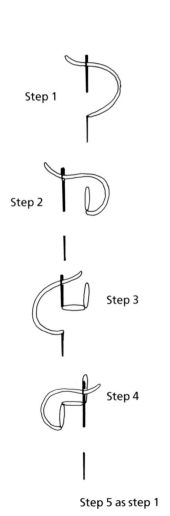

Step 1

Step 2

Step 3

Step 4

Step 5 as step 1

92 Insertion stitch
A useful and simple stitch for making a decorative join.

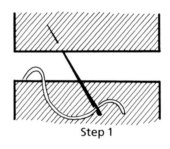

Step 1

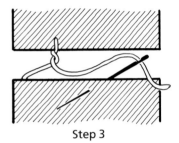

Step 3

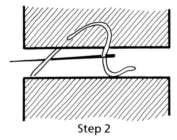

Step 2

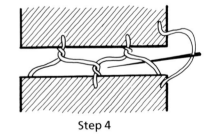

Step 4

93 Long and short stitch
Outline the shape to be filled with a split or backstitch. Row 1 is worked over the outline, and in subsequent rows the needle should come up and split the stitches of the previous row.

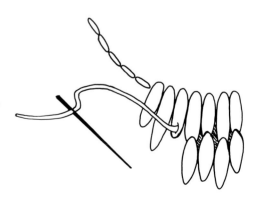

94 Mosaic stitch *(pulled work)*
*Blocks of four satin stitches are
arranged in a square, worked
over three threads, with a cross
stitch filling, contained in a
box of four straight stitches.*

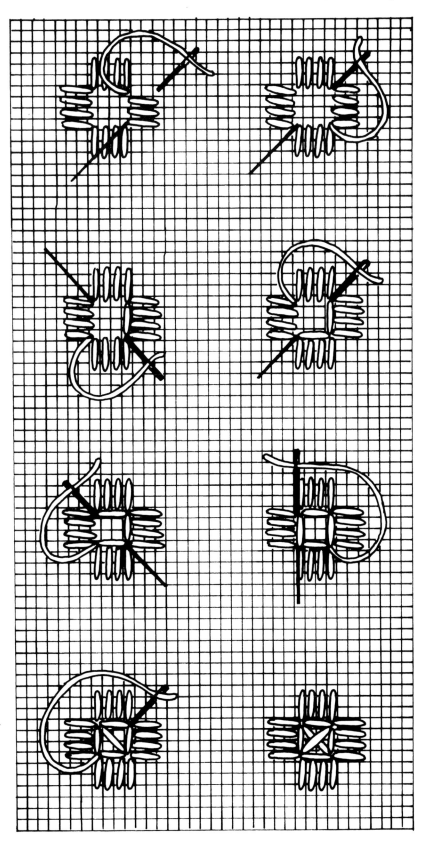

95 Slip stitch
Slip your needle through the folded edges of the fabric, moving from one side to the other alternately.

96 *and* **97 Squared edge stitch** *(pulled work)*
A neat, strong finish for an evenweave fabric.

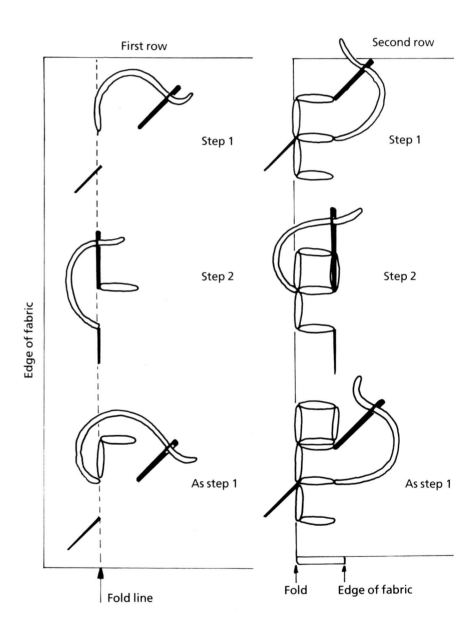

First row — Second row

Step 1 — Step 1

Step 2 — Step 2

As step 1 — As step 1

Edge of fabric

Fold line

Fold   Edge of fabric

Stay stitching *(machining)*
This is a line of machine stitching, worked on the seam allowance, just beyond the stitch line. It prevents stretching and reinforces seam allowances, which have to be clipped as far as the stitching (not illustrated).

98 Stem stitch *(smocking)*

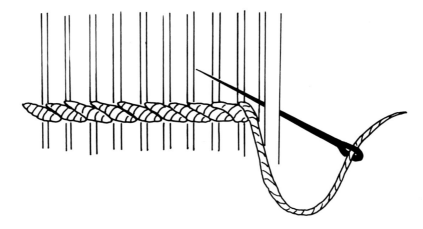

99 Tailor's tacks
Use a double length of rough cotton to work these loose loops through double fabric. Cut the threads between the opened layers of fabric, leaving marker tufts on each layer.

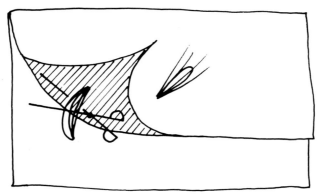

100 Trammed tent stitch
A long thread is held down by the slanting tent stitches, which are worked over it.

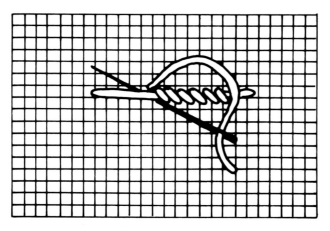

101 Trellis stitch *(smocking)*

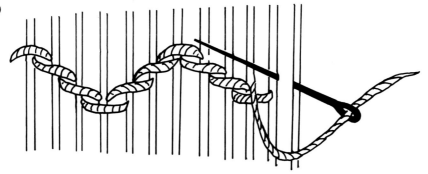

Useful Materials and Tools

◆

Fabric support and interfacing

Some fabrics require extra support. We have used three types:

1 Iron-on Vilene
This is a non-woven fusible interfacing, used to support gloving leather and fabric to prevent stretching and to give body.

2 Sew-in Vilene
This interfacing comes in several weights and can be used to stiffen and give body; for example, when using a soft fabric to make up a bag with a firm outline.

3 Stitch and Tear
A non-permanent support, helpful for obtaining neat stitching with the machine on thin or stretchy fabrics, such as silk or leather. It is torn away when the stitching is complete.

Domette

A soft, fluffy interfacing.

Foam

In many of the projects a thin layer of foam has been used as an interfacing to give body and softness with a neat appearance. You should be able to buy this from your local market or from an upholsterer.

Adhesives

Adhesives are essential for holding seam allowances flat when working with leather. They are also useful for holding sections in position while they are being sewn, especially fabrics that would otherwise show pin marks. We have used Pritt Stick, Unibond PVA adhesive, Evostik Impact 2 and Spray Mount. Always use as little as possible.

Masking Tape

This is useful for binding raw edges of canvas when it is worked in the hand.

Fabric Paints

A wide range of fabric paints is available. We have used Deka silk paints throughout the book. They are easy to handle, need only a hot iron for fixing, and are bright and colourfast. For spraying the paints on to the fabric, a diffuser, obtainable from any art shop, was used.

Embroidery Frames

1 Tambour frames are essential for free machine embroidery and should be the wooden type, which can be tightened with a screw. The spring type is suitable only for hand work. Tambour frames are not suitable for canvas work.

2 Tapestry – or slate – frames should be used for canvas work. Small pieces can be worked in the hand.

Sewing Machines

Any sewing machines can be used for embroidery, but elaborate automatic stitches are found only on modern machines. We have been very happy to use the latest computerized machine from Pfaff. Many of the projects in this book make use of zipper foot and leather foot attachments.

Handbag Frames

A large number of different types of metal handbag frames is available. We have used spring purse frames, twist-knob, sew-in frames and press-in frames.

You may want to explore the possibilities of using wooden or plastic frames. A search around flea markets and antique shops may yield an exciting find, around which you may design an original bag (diagrams 102 and 103).

102 *and* **103** *Two drawings showing ideas for using wooden frames.*

Fasteners

Try to use suitable fasteners for your bag and ones that will give a professional finish and be secure. We have used three types: press-studs, magnetic press-studs and turn locks.

The press-studs are fixed with two prongs, which pierce some of the fabric layers and are backed with a metal plate. The turn lock is fixed in a similar way, but pierces all layers and needs a punched hole to allow the swivel to protrude.

Zip Fasteners

Frequently found on all types of bags, zip fasteners can close pockets as well as top openings. According to the bag design, they can be sewn in by hand or machine. The zip should be strong enough for the purpose of the bag and be in keeping with both the style and the fabric. If you find it difficult to obtain the length you need, zip fastening, sold by the yard or metre, can be cut to the correct size. Allow 1in (2.5cm) for security and stitch across it firmly 1in (2.5cm) from the bottom.

Trimmings

Swivel trigger- or dog lead clips are often used to attach handles straps or cord to bags. They are available in many different sizes.

Metal eyelets are available in many different sizes and finishes. They usually come with a fitting tool. It is advisable to buy two or three more than you need for your bag so that you can practise fitting them on some spare material.

Rings and D-rings

These are a useful and decorative way to attach straps and drawstrings.

Marker pens

There are a number of marker pens on the market, both air- and water-soluble, and also indelible. It is vital that you use the right pen for the job.

OPPOSITE

A collection of antique bags. Top: *a satin evening clutch bag from the 1920s, sold by Fortnum and Mason and decorated with fine, hand-stitched leather appliqué;* second from top: *a rectangular wallet/purse of silk satin, possibly French and dating from the early nineteenth century, which is decorated with tambour work;* centre left: *a nineteenth-century miser's purse of crocheted silk with steel rings;* centre right: *a circular beaded purse with a silver frame;* below left: *a beaded bag; and* below right: *a nineteenth-century bag worked entirely in rococo stitch with handmade tassels and cords.*

Learning from the Past

B Y NOW we hope that you have made some lovely purses and bags and that you are ready to design your own work. Designers have always drawn on the past for their inspiration. For centuries, bags and purses have been highly decorated and popular objects. We know, for instance, of gifts of purses made to Queen Elizabeth I in the sixteenth century. During this period bags were small and square, made mostly of linen and richly embellished with silver thread, elaborate tassels and bobbles. They were drawn up with plaited cords of metal threads and silk. These lovely articles often contained gifts of money, perfume or sweets. The idea of a bag as a present is an attractive one, especially if it contains a small surprise as well.

Collections of antique bags are owned by most museums and these are well worth visiting with a sketch book and pen, even a camera, should photography be allowed. Once you begin to look, ideas usually come thick and fast and it is a rewarding experience to discover and study the work of those who loved and made embroidery in former times and whose work is the inheritance of today's designers and embroiderers.

Even your own loft may yield some forgotten treasures. If these are now too fragile or too old fashioned to use in their present state, they can still be good starting points for a modern interpretation. Parts of the bag may remain usable, such as the frame or fasteners and trimmings. The decoration on an old silver frame, probably from Holland, suggested the design for decorating a new bag to replace the old one (see diagram 104). When you take an antique bag apart, look carefully at the way it was constructed. Make notes and drawings as you unpick. Pay special attention to the inside, as these are often very decorative (see diagram 105).

Another useful exercise, and one which most people could do at some stage, is to dismantle a discarded modern handbag and to work out exactly how it was made. If it happened to be a favourite bag and is in a simple style and seems easy to reproduce, take a paper pattern from it and make it up in calico. If it works, you can design some embroidery for it and carry on from there. You will have an original bag; and one that you know you will like.

104 *Drawings from the old Dutch silver frame in the photograph on page 122, a design source for a new bag*

105 *A drawing of an Edwardian bag, before it was taken apart and the frame used for the bag on page 122*

106 *Some motifs, drawn from a piece of eighteenth-century embroidery, probably Spanish*

107 *The butterfly motif from the piece of eighteenth-century embroidery, which was worked in long and short stitch, has been drawn and developed into a variety of formal and informal patterns. These are shown fitting into a small purse shape.*

OPPOSITE

Old frames for new bags. Top left: *an antique ivory frame with a new pouch in wool with drawn thread and pulled work and beaded tassels;* centre right: *a smocked and beaded velvet pouch attached to a circular, expanding, brass frame, both velvet and frame dating from the 1920s;* centre left: *a late Victorian frame with a canvas pouch worked in* or nué, *the aluminium threads couched down with stranded cotton; and* below right: *an antique silver frame.*

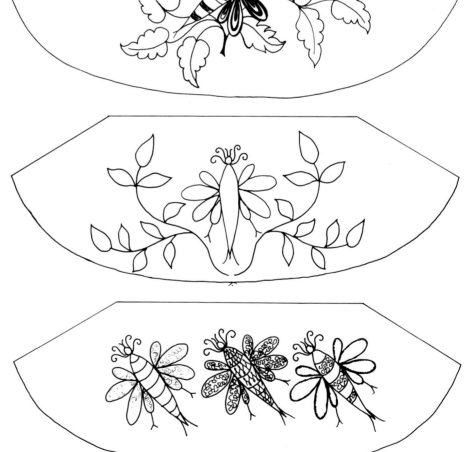

108 *The butterfly motif from diagram 107 has been overlapped to give various abstract patterns.*

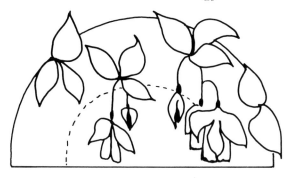

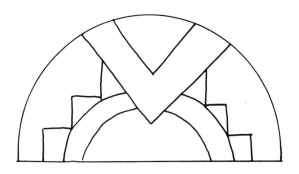

109 *Different patterns can be fitted into the same shapes. See page 51. Experiment before making your final decision.*

110 *The rose design has been curved to fit into the shape of a small purse.*

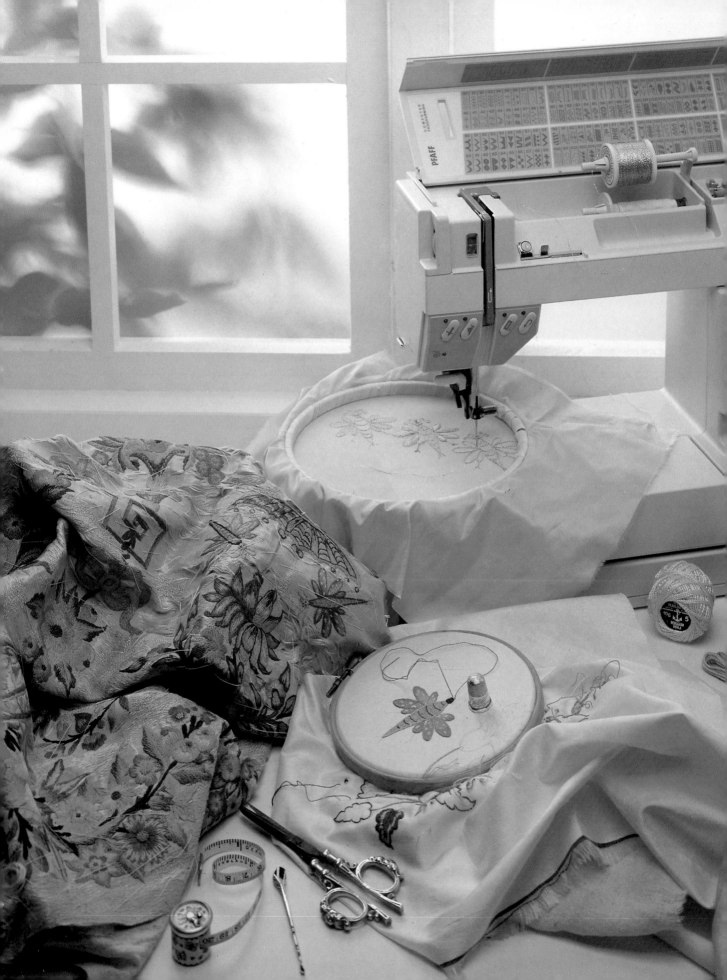

Suppliers

◆

UNITED KINGDOM
C. W. Pittard & Co Ltd
Sherborne Road
Yeovil
Somerset BA21 5BA

Suppliers of fine leathers of all kinds

Milner Leather
Corris Craft Centre
Machynlleth
Powys SY20 9RF
Tel: (065473) 618

Leather, clasps, magnetic press-studs,
purse frames, spring frames

Peter Davis (Silks) Ltd
59-61 Gee Street
Goswell Road
London EC1V 3RT
Tel: 071-253 9677

Suppliers of handbag frames and linings
for leather goods

UNITED STATES
Markann Manufacturing Corp.
69 Warren St
New Rochelle
NY 10801
Tel: 914-636-7500

Manufacturers of pre-finished
accessories for needlepoint and cross
stitch. Slip-in totes, handbags, evening
bags, clutch and cosmetic bags, eyeglass
cases, briefcases, racquetball,
paddleball and tennis racquet covers.
Golf club covers, identity tags, pre-
bound belting, bellpulls and trims

The Berry Patch
P.O. Box 6000
Sandhills Industrial Park
Pinehurst
NC 28374
Tel: 919-944-7626

Counted thread supplies include: books
big and little, colour cover leaflets; kits –
beginners, Christmas ornaments, Easter
eggs, totes, purses, greeting cards. Also
framing hoops, cards, needles, bag
handles, Dylite forms. Candlewick
supplies and designs

Bunka Embroidery International, Inc.
5073 Dorchester Rd
P.O. Box 10321
Charleston
SC 29411
Tel: 803-552-0440

Matsuhato brand, Tokyo Bunka brand,
Bunka Embroidery International Inc.
brand, Bunka embroidery kits, working
frames, punch needles, threads,
brushes, trimming clippers, basic
English Bunka embroidery instruction
book, tacks in bags, tacks with puller,
thread colour books

Jacmore Needlecraft Inc.
2337 McDonald Avenue
Brooklyn
NY 11223
Tel: 212-336-6262

Bellpull hardware, handbag handles,
metallic threads, pre-mounted items,
belt buckles, wood novelties and
knitting bags

OPPOSITE
Using old designs. A
fragment of an eighteenth-
century embroidered fabric
copied (in the foreground) by
hand in long and short stitch
and interpreted in free
embroidery on a modern
domestic sewing machine.

127

Index